Also by Tiger Woods

How I Play Golf

The 1997 Masters

My Story

Tiger Woods
With Lorne Rubenstein

GRAND CENTRAL
PUBLISHING

LARGE PRINT

Grand Central Publishing
Hachette Book Group
1290 Avenue of the Americas, New York, NY 10104
grandcentralpublishing.com
twitter.com/grandcentralpub

First Edition: March 2017

Grand Central Publishing is a division of Hachette Book Group, Inc. The Grand Central Publishing name and logo is a trademark of Hachette Book Group, Inc.

The publisher is not responsible for websites (or their content) that are not owned by the publisher.

The Hachette Speakers Bureau provides a wide range of authors for speaking events. To find out more, go to www.hachettespeakersbureau.com or call (866) 376-6591.

Library of Congress Cataloging-in-Publication Data has been applied for.

ISBNs: 978-1-4555-4358-8 (hardcover), 978-1-4555-7150-5 (ebook), 978-1-5387-4397-3 (large print)

Printed in the United States of America

LSC-C

10   9   8   7   6   5   4   3   2   1

Contents

The 1997 Masters

Chapter One

Turning It Around

It takes a minute or two to walk from the ninth green to the tenth tee at the Augusta National Golf Club, and I needed that time to think. I'd just shot 40 on the front nine of the 1997 Masters, my first as a professional after playing as an amateur the two previous years. Jack Nicklaus said after a practice round with me in 1996 that the course was so suited to my game that I could win more green jackets than he and Arnold Palmer combined. Nicklaus won six Masters, and Palmer four. I felt when I first played the course that it was perfect for me. When I heard from the media that Jack predicted I could win the Masters so many times, I wondered whether he knew what an astronomical number it was. Did he realize what it would take to get to that number? It was an awfully nice compliment, but also such a big number that it was pretty well impossible for me to contemplate.

I figured Jack said that because he had seen that I drove the ball long enough that I could overpower the course. If I birdied each of the four par-5s, then the course was effectively a par-68 rather than 72 for me. I could reach every par-5 in two, and I'd be hitting wedges into most of the par-4s. Yet I'd just made four bogeys and no birdies on the front nine. I hit my opening tee shot high and left into the trees and bogeyed the hole, not exactly the start I wanted. I hit three more drives high and left into the trees. What was going on? I had to make a nice putt for bogey on the ninth hole just to finish the front side 4 over par. But I knew one thing above all as I walked to the tenth tee: My start wasn't going to finish me.

Most people would say that nobody recovers from a first-nine 40 at the Masters. I'd learn later that the media were already writing me off, even as I was making my way to the back nine. I'd played only nine holes and had bad starts in final matches while winning three straight U.S. Juniors and then three straight U.S. Amateurs. Then I announced in August 1996 that I was turning pro and leaving Stanford after my sophomore year. Now I was a professional golfer, and I had quite a challenge ahead of me.

"Hello, world," I'd said at a press conference the day after I announced that I was turning pro. I had just won my third straight U.S. Amateur, where I was five down after the morning round of the thirty-six-hole final match against Steve Scott, a University of Florida golfer. I was two down with three to play in the match, but tied it up and won on the second extra hole. I was a confident golfer, and I'd proven to myself that I could find my game even when things weren't going well. Still, two-time U.S. Open champion Curtis Strange, who was working for ABC, had asked what I expected when I teed it up as a professional. I said I entered every tournament to win. Strange told me, "You'll learn." I suppose the skepticism was understandable, but I knew what I was capable of.

I then won two of my first eight PGA Tour events as a professional, and therefore qualified to play the 1997 PGA Tour full-time, exempt from qualifying for tournaments. The hype surrounding me by the end of 1996, and going into the Masters, was intense. I was having trouble handling all the attention. Writers followed me when I walked to my car. Television cameras were in my face. I was being asked personal questions that had nothing to do with golf. That was the deal, and I realized I'd better adjust quickly.

This was my new life as a professional, and there were plenty of perks—such as the Nike deal that I'd signed, flying on private airplanes, and, ten years later, flying in my own airplane. But more than anything, I loved golf and competing. I needed to cope with the magnifying glass trained on me all the time. I found it stifling at times, but as Arnold Palmer told me, the attention was going to be there, and it would be unrelenting. If the glare was magnified that much more at the Masters, how would I perform?

I didn't play well at all, not at the start anyway. I shot that 40, and I was bewildered and furious as I walked to the tenth tee. I was trying to think about what had just happened. I needed to figure out what went so wrong on the front nine. Security guards and, beyond them, "patrons," as Augusta National prefers to refer to spectators at the Masters, flanked me as I walked. I decided that my backswing got too long on the front nine, and I didn't like that feeling. I didn't like it when my backswing even got to parallel. I got out of sync then, and I had to get back on the right path to the ball by using my arms alone, rather than allowing my lower body to carry them through. Swinging that way meant I had to depend on my timing, which wasn't reliable.

I wanted my swing to feel tight. This provided me the control I craved. But by *control* I didn't mean that I wasn't swinging freely. I could make an uninhibited swing at my best, without mechanical thoughts. I wanted that feeling. Maybe, as a golfer, I lived for it, especially when it mattered the most, when I had to produce a swing that wins. I had learned as a young golfer that I wanted to be in a position where my winning depended on my making the shot when I needed to, rather than winning because another player made a mistake. The feeling of coming through was intoxicating.

Twenty years later, as I think about that walk and the issue with my backswing, I know that there was so much more than technique involved. I was looking for the feelings I had in my swing only the Friday of the week before the Masters, when, with my friend and fellow professional Mark O'Meara, I had shot 59 at the Isleworth Golf & Country Club in Orlando. I lived there, and so did Marko. I took a cart and listened to music while I went along. We started on the back nine. I played one nine-hole stretch in 10 under par and took a few bucks off him. My swing felt fluid from start to finish; the game felt easy.

Along the way, in midafternoon, we had quite a surprise. On the third hole, a par-5, we hit our drives around the corner. I teed off and was going to hit a three-iron in to the par-5. I looked out around the corner and saw a white plume. The space shuttle

Columbia had just launched from the Kennedy Space Center. We saw the whole thing, and it was chilling. I'd just moved to Isleworth, and had never seen the shuttle. We sat in our carts and watched as the booster came off to where there wasn't any exhaust. I had been interested in the space program since I was a kid, and I often read about NASA's missions. Sitting there in the cart, I was in awe; just to think, scientists were making this happen. What an accomplishment. There I was, playing golf while seven astronauts had just taken off in a space shuttle that, I would learn later, weighed 259,000 pounds and would reach an apogee of 188 miles— the point in its orbit that the satellite would be the farthest from the center of the earth. I liked reading about science, and suddenly we had come across the shuttle. I felt both small by comparison to space travel, and in awe of what man could achieve. I felt exhilarated sitting there.

We played again the next day. I shot 32 on the front nine, birdied the tenth hole, and made a hole in one on the eleventh. Marko didn't say a word after the hole in one. Suddenly he drove off in his cart. "Huh?" I thought. I assumed he had had enough. It was his way of saying, *"This is crazy. You shoot 59, and now you make a hole in one. I'm outta here."* I followed in my cart.

Something else happened in the week before the Masters that helped my confidence. Arnold Palmer had invited me to play at the Bay Hill Club & Lodge, which he owned. I'd admired Arnold for years, especially his attacking, go-for-broke attitude and the way he managed to not only cope with all the attention his game and friendly nature brought him, but to welcome it. I'd sought him out for advice on these matters, and he was always willing to sit down to talk with me. Before I turned pro, I picked his brain about the world of professional golf, what it takes to get there and succeed, and how to handle the attention that comes with the sport. He was a great mentor as I was entering the new world of professional golf.

At Bay Hill, in what was called the Shootout, Arnold, who was then sixty-seven, played with his buddies every day at noon. This time, I was there playing with him in a group, and it was exciting. We had a match for $100, and I closed him out on the seventeenth hole. But Arnold being Arnold, he wasn't about to say we shouldn't have another wager on the last hole. So, we played the eighteenth for double or nothing. I was miles by him off the tee after hitting three-wood. He hit driver, driver—even though the second shot is one of the most dangerous shots in golf because of the way the green wraps around the lake in front—and he finished in the back bunker. I then hit eight-iron to the green. Arnold got up and down for par, I missed my birdie putt, and so we halved the hole. That was pure Arnold. He had no give-up in him. He believed it was possible to turn things around, whatever the circumstances. Maybe one of the best examples of his attitude came in the 1960 Masters, when he birdied the last two holes to win by a shot over Ken Venturi. He knew he had to birdie the holes, because Venturi was already finished.

* * *

I was fortunate to get to know Arnold before I turned professional. Eventually, I won the Arnold Palmer Invitational at Bay Hill eight times, and it was a thrill to see him standing behind the eighteenth green where he waited to congratulate the winner. I was sad when he died on September 25, 2016, and I thought of all those times behind the eighteenth green. Arnold meant so much to the game, and I'll never forget our friendship and his counsel to me over the years. Looking back, I know that he fired me up the week before the Masters.

Then, at Augusta, after the match with Arnold and shooting 59 at Isleworth the next day, I played practice rounds with Mo—I called Mark O'Meara Marko, Mo, Mark. I also played nine holes with Seve Ballesteros and José María Olazábal on the Monday of Masters week. Seve, a two-time Masters champion, had the best hands in the game, and Ollie—as everybody called him—was also a short-game master. Seve showed me a variety of shots around Augusta's complicated greens. I wanted to learn from the best, from former Masters winners. That was why I made sure to play practice rounds at Augusta with Seve and Ollie, and with other winners such as Nicklaus, Palmer, Raymond Floyd, and Fred Couples.

The first round was approaching, and while I was confident in my swing, my putting was off. Still, I'd never have believed I would shoot 40 on the front side. I was having a problem with my speed, and speed determines line. I couldn't feel comfortable on the greens during practice, and I couldn't make any headway. The night before the opening round, I decided to ask my father, Earl, for his advice. Nobody knew me better than Pop. But he wasn't well. He had had a quadruple bypass in the 1980s, and then had to go back into the hospital while I was playing the Tour Championship in Atlanta at the end of the 1996 season. I couldn't concentrate after spending the night in the hospital with my father, worrying about him, and I shot 78 in the second round. He then had a triple bypass only a month and a half before the Masters. I flew out from Orlando to see him at the UCLA hospital, and, watching the monitor beside his bed, I saw that Pop had flatlined. He told me later that, in that moment, he felt a surge of warmth, and felt he was walking into the light. But he decided he didn't want to go to the light. "All I felt was warmth," he told me. "Do I go to the warmth or not? I made a conscious decision not to go to the warmth." He survived, but his doctor didn't want him traveling to the Masters. He didn't want him to fly.

Pop said, "Screw that. I'm going to watch my son." He flew to Augusta on Tuesday of Masters week. He was staying in the same house with me, as was our custom. He had no energy. He was with it half the time, and half the time he seemed dazed, and fell asleep frequently. Now, the evening before the first round, he was in bed. I needed help. I grabbed three balls and got into my putting posture as he lay there in bed, and asked him if he saw anything.

He did, and told me, "Your hands are too low. Lift them up. Get that little arch in your hands like you always do." I had to adjust my left-hand position and my posture to accommodate the change. This meant that my forward press on the putter was different, but I knew Pop was right. I made the modifications he suggested, and tightened my left-hand grip. Now I felt ready for the opening round. But I still shot 40, and I'd putted well to do that. My putting wasn't the problem. Pop had solved that.

But my feel wasn't there. I was upset that I'd made so many bad swings, and, worse, that the feel of a good swing had deserted me. I was hot inside. Then, just before I stepped on the tenth tee, I let go of that anger, and calmed myself. I was thinking of the feeling I had the week before at Isleworth, when I hit one perfect shot after another. The feeling washed over me. My heart rate slowed. I felt the motion of my swing, and the tightness I wanted, the sense of controlled power through the ball. I felt free. There were sixty-three holes left in the Masters, as my caddie, Mike "Fluff" Cowan, reminded me while we walked to the tenth tee. I relinquished the forced, conscious control I had inadvertently exerted over my swing and game on the front nine. That was no way to play—to really *play* golf. I needed the freedom that comes with *playing*. By *playing* I mean I didn't need to force things, or to overthink the swing. I was executing the old idea that you can't think and swing at the same time.

It was calming to have Fluff at my side. He had caddied for Peter Jacobsen for eighteen years, and was with him for six wins. But Peter had been playing hurt, and had to withdraw from the PGA Championship the previous August. He was going to take time off. I got wind of that, and I called Peter for permission to ask Fluff to caddie for me. He said that was fine, and so I called Fluff on my way back from winning the U.S. Amateur to ask if he would caddie for me. Fluff being Fluff, he made sure I knew that his work with me might last only until Peter was healthy enough to tee it up again. I admired his sense of loyalty.

Fluff was nearing fifty, and he was the original free spirit. I had never met somebody so into the Grateful Dead; he was a Deadhead and had been to many of the band's concerts. We hadn't talked much about the Dead since he started caddying for me when I turned pro; what did I know about the band, and anyway, I wasn't interested. Their music wasn't my music. I was into hip-hop. But I did appreciate Fluff's laid-back demeanor and that very little on the course got to him. He'd caddied for me in all three tournaments I had won on tour. In addition to the two I had won in 1996, I won the Mercedes Championships to start 1997—and he always seemed to know what to say. He was a psychologist as much as a caddie, simply by being himself. He helped settle me down with his "go with the flow" approach. The last thing I needed as I went from nine to ten was tension in the air because of my lousy play on the front nine. Tension and Fluff didn't go together.

Now I was on the tenth tee. I pulled the two-iron out of my bag. Fluff liked the choice of club. I blistered the two-iron down the fairway. There, right there, that was it. That was the feeling I had at Isleworth. My pace picked up as I walked to my ball, and from a perfect position in the fairway, I hit an eight-iron within fifteen feet of the hole, and made the birdie putt. "Okay, this is it," I told myself. "I'll be fine." I knew it, from that one swing on the tenth tee. Sometimes in golf everything can turn around, for better or worse, with one swing. This was the swing that was going to turn it around for me. I was playing a very short course for me, and I'd made my Isleworth 59 swing. Here we go.

I didn't miss a shot the rest of the way. After making birdie on ten I pitched in from just over the green on the par-3 twelfth for birdie. I birdied the par-5 thirteenth, eagled the par-5 fifteenth, then birdied the seventeenth hole. I was into it, and was hitting the ball long and where I wanted to hit it. I hit pitching wedge into the fifteenth to set up the eagle. I was dialed in. My birdie on seventeen came after I hit a lob wedge from eighty-seven yards right over the top of the flag, to twelve feet from the hole. My birdie putt on eighteen to shoot 29 on the back nine slid just past the right edge, and so I shot a 6-under-par 30 on the back side. Forty. Thirty. Seventy. Three shots out of the lead.

There was still plenty of light. I went to the practice range to ingrain the feel of the swing I made on the back nine for the second round. My swing coach, Butch Harmon, accompanied me as I followed one sweet shot with another. Neither Fluff nor Butchie—which was how I usually referred to him—needed to say much. I was okay.

Chapter Two

Amateur Days at the Masters

My first significant Masters memory was from 1986, when I was ten years old and Jack Nicklaus was making a run toward his sixth green jacket. My dad and I had played nine holes on the morning of the last round, which had become our annual routine. We came home, and I was watching the last round on television with my parents soon after Jack started the back nine.

He began the final round tied for ninth, four shots behind Greg Norman, and was even for the day until he birdied the ninth. No big deal. He wasn't really in contention. But then he birdied the tenth and eleventh holes before making bogey on the twelfth. His move appeared stalled, except that this was Jack

Nicklaus. He birdied the thirteenth, parred fourteen, and hit his drive to the top of the hill on fifteen. That was where his presence registered with me.

Jack was at the top of the hill looking down at the green over the pond in front, and his son, Jackie Jr., was caddying for him. Jack asked his son, "How far do you think a three would go here?" Jackie thought he was asking how far he would hit a three-iron. But Jack was asking his son what he thought an eagle three would do for him in terms of where he stood in the tournament. Jack was four shots behind Seve Ballesteros at the time. Jackie handed his dad a four-iron on fifteen, and Jack hit a perfect shot over the water in front of the green that finished twelve feet from the hole.

What I remember about this is the way Jack reacted to the shot. He raised his arms after the ball stopped on the green, with his fists in the air: kind of little fist pumps, nothing over the top. Still, I wondered why he was reacting that way. He'd hit the shot he wanted, but the hole wasn't over. His reaction made no sense to me, as a ten-year-old. I was baffled that you would react that way when the hole wasn't done. I could compare it to a pitcher who has just thrown his two best fastballs, it's an 0-2 count, and he's showing how pleased he is. But the at bat wasn't over. The pitcher hasn't struck out the batter. Jack hadn't finished the hole. But of course Jack made his eagle putt on the fifteenth, walking it in as the ball neared the hole.

In 2016, at the Champions Dinner that takes place every Tuesday night of Masters week, I was sitting with Jack and Arnold. It was neat, fourteen green jackets next to each other. Jack had his six, Arnold had won four, and I'd won four. I was talking to Jack about the thirtieth anniversary of his win in 1986, and I asked him, "Jack, do you realize what my highlight of the week was?" He said, "I have no idea. What was that?"

I told him that I'd seen him do something I'd never seen anyone do in golf. He asked what I meant. "Well," I said, "you celebrated on fifteen after your second shot with both fists up in the air. I got that you hit exactly the shot you wanted, and gave yourself a chance to make eagle. But I'd never seen anyone celebrate before they finished the hole." The hole wasn't done. I asked Jack why he was celebrating.

Jack didn't really give me an answer. But he did tell me about the circumstances of the shot, and the question he had asked Jackie about how far a three would go there. I laughed and said, "Jack, I've heard that story a bunch of times." But celebrating before the hole was over? I'd never seen that, and didn't understand it while watching as a ten-year-old.

It was a few years after 1986 before I had more understanding of the game and could begin to see why Jack would react like he did. He felt the moment and the situation. He did what he needed to do to put himself in position to win the Masters. He wasn't thinking about winning. He was thinking only about the shot, and what he needed to do. He wasn't getting ahead of himself, which can easily happen.

Jack, after he made eagle on fifteen, then hit a five-iron within three feet of the hole on the sixteenth and made that putt to get to 8 under for the tournament. He left himself a birdie putt of ten feet on the seventeenth green, and he reacted as the ball approached the center of the hole. His left heel came up, and his right hand came off the grip. He was staring at the ball and stepped forward as it was about to fall. His left hand and arm came straight up while his right arm was at his side, straight down, as the ball fell. Jack's mouth was wide open, as CBS's Verne Lundquist, unknown to Jack at the time but legendary since, proclaimed: "Yessir." The hole was over. Jack had gotten to 9 under, which was where he finished after he tapped in for par on the last hole.

His reactions over those last holes of the 1986 Masters made an impression on me because they were spontaneous, and they showed me how much of yourself you have to put into a shot. Harvey Penick said you have to believe the shot you're about to play is the most important thing in the world, at that moment. It's just a golf shot, true, but at that moment, it's more important than breathing. You have to be so involved in it that nothing can penetrate your concentration. If the shot comes off, you might react in a way that you wouldn't have expected, or that will surprise you when you think about it.

Along these lines, I think of my reaction when I holed a twenty-five-foot birdie putt on the eighteenth green the last day to win the 2008 Arnold Palmer Invitational at Bay Hill by a shot over Bart Bryant. When the ball fell, I whipped my cap off my head with my right hand and flung it on the ground—I mean, I flung it, hard. I had no recollection of doing that and didn't know where my cap was. You can't script such a reaction.

Jack's reaction there on fifteen at the '86 Masters has stayed with me, because I learned something watching him that Sunday afternoon. The game can bring intense satisfaction, and it's worth working as hard as you can to maybe put yourself into a situation where everything depends on you hitting the right shot. Jack was forty-six, and I was only ten, and I couldn't put it into words then. But I wanted to be where he was, and doing what he was doing.

* * *

By the time I watched the 1986 Masters, I had been playing real golf for six or seven years. By "real golf," I mean counting my score in a tournament. I finished second in a pitch, putt, and drive—an early version, I suppose, of Augusta National's Drive, Chip, & Putt Championship that started qualifying tournaments in 2013 for the 2014 Masters. It brings kids who qualify to the club for the finals on the Sunday before the Masters. At the tournament I played, I won a trophy that was almost as big as I was. I thought that was the neatest thing ever.

That was hardly my first exposure to golf, though. We were living in Cypress, a city of about forty thousand people in Southern California. It was a mostly white, middle-class neighborhood. Some of the residents weren't happy that a mixed-race family had moved in, and threw things at the house—lemons, limes, rocks. Dad had two sons and a daughter from a first marriage, and they told me about the incident. My half brothers, Kevin and Earl Jr., went over to the house where the people who took exception to our moving in lived, knocked on the door, and had a little discussion to clear up the situation. They didn't throw rocks at the house anymore.

Pop had served two tours of duty in the U.S.

Army, in Vietnam. He was a Green Beret, and he was one tough man. Pop had met Mom when he was on an information assignment where she was working. They married and first lived in Brooklyn, where he was a lieutenant colonel stationed at Fort Hamilton. Pop was invited to play a game of golf, and he liked it immediately because it provided such a challenge. He was a skilled baseball player, and he loved that sport. But golf gave him another outlet. When he and Mom moved to Cypress, he was able to play at the Navy Golf Course.

My mother, Tida, hadn't been in the United States very long after moving here from Thailand. In Thailand, there's not much, if any, of a melting pot. And now that she was living in the U.S., she quickly saw a side of American culture that was hurtful, and she never forgot that such treatment was possible. She toughened up. Mom was, and still is, strong and feisty. As we said in our family, my mom was the hand, and my dad was the voice. I could negotiate with him, but not with my mom. There was no middle ground with Mom. You were right or you were wrong. She would tell me that I had to be home five minutes before the streetlights came on in front of our house. If I was one second late, that meant one day of restrictions—no going to the park for me. I didn't always get the message—or, I should say, I ignored it—and so the restrictions continued for me every time I messed up. It was my responsibility to get home in time. If not, I knew what was coming.

Earlier, at home, my dad set up a practice area in the garage, and he sat me down in a high chair to watch him hit balls into a net. I was only nine months old. Although I don't remember my dad hitting balls there, apparently I didn't take my eyes off him. Something about the contact between the clubface and the ball, or the thwack when the ball hit the net, must have appealed to me.

I do remember putting in the garage for hours as I got a bit older. Pop had put down the worst-looking, and worn, carpet on the floor, but it had what I would call lanes that were the same width as the head of a putter. I wanted to make sure that my putter moved away from the ball and inside the lane, then back to where I would hit the ball, and then moved inside and away from the lane again. That was the start of what I like to think of as a stroke that resembled Ben Crenshaw's—inside the line going back, through the line at impact, and then back inside the line. I've never wanted to take the putter straight back and straight through. That made no sense to me, because the shaft of a putter is on an angle. It's not straight up, ninety degrees from the ball. A pendulum stroke is fine if you're perfectly ninety degrees vertical, but what putter is like that? If the shaft is on an arc, then the stroke should also be on an arc. The putter swings. It's a stroke, but it's also a swing.

Subconsciously, I learned that in the garage on the ratty piece of carpet. The colors were almost blinding, yellow, green, and orange. It was putrid. My dad never used it, but I putted for hours on it. I putted to music by Run-DMC. Their sound and the beat fired me up, and I still listen to them to this day. My dad was a big fan of classical jazz, though. He wasn't too thrilled with hip-hop. His music was John Coltrane, Miles Davis, and Charlie Parker. When he followed me in tournaments, he would often take a break on his seat stick and listen to jazz tapes on his Walkman. Sometimes he fell asleep. If I passed his way again, or if he caught up to me, he knew right away how I had been doing by the way I was walking and the look on my face.

I had so many good times with my dad on the course when I was a kid. My parents were really good at encouraging me in the game without pushing me or making me feel bad when I played poorly. My job was to try my best. The result didn't matter, because I would learn from it—whether it was a good result or not. I was lucky that way. My mom drove me to all my junior tournaments, throughout Southern

California, before I got my license. The courses were often an hour or more away. My responsibility was to make sure we got to the course on time. I learned how to read a map, what time we should leave, how long it would take us to get to the course, and what the alternate routes were. If we weren't early, we were late, because I had to warm up. Mom walked every hole with me and kept score. We talked about the round on the way home—when I didn't fall asleep, that is.

My nature on the course was to get into my little world. My dad was different when we played. He didn't take up golf until he was forty-two, yet he got down around a scratch handicap. The game fascinated him, but he wasn't going to subdue his nature to play it. Pop was outgoing and talked all the time while playing. That was just who he was. I approached the game differently. I could talk all day if I wanted to, but I learned early that I played my best golf when I cut off any conversation and got zoned in for the shot. More than anything, though, I liked to be on the course with my dad, often only the two of us. It was peaceful when we played on the Navy course in the evening.

All these years later, I can see the trees on the course. I remember them from when I played there, especially a tree on the right at one spot. It was a nine-iron for me to get there, and it became a wedge when I grew up a bit. When I got out of school, I would arrive at the course in the evening. We didn't have a whole lot of time to get some golf in, and very little during the winter. Nevertheless, those evenings to me were connected to golfing with my dad. Early on, I had to sneak onto the course, because you weren't allowed on it until you were ten years old. I did notice that white kids under ten played, but I wasn't allowed to mix with them.

Anyway, I wanted to be out there with Pop, and if I had to sneak onto the course, so be it. I did that starting when I was four years old. My mom dropped me off. I hopped into a ditch and scrambled to the other side. The clubhouse was up above, which meant no one could see me. My dad got a cart. I walked out past the first hole, and past the second, and I laid down under the bridge on the third hole. I was trying to be in total disguise, so I could blend into the environment. To do that, I put rocks and vegetation around me when I snuck on. I hid my golf bag under the rocks, and then I'd hear my dad in his cart. "Hey, you there?" Yup, coming up. As I think back, I would have played in the dark, that's how much I loved those times I spent with my dad.

I liked playing other sports as well, including baseball, football, and basketball, just for fun, although I was always competitive. I also enjoyed cycling and skateboarding. But something had to give. So, as I started junior high, Mom and Pop told me I had to choose one sport. Golf was obviously special to me given how much time I wanted to spend practicing and playing. My mom told me, and she meant it, that I couldn't play until I did my homework. That didn't leave time for the other sports in my life, so I chose to focus on golf.

I didn't interact much with kids on the course during casual rounds, although I played with them in tournaments. Whatever racism I felt—and it was there—I learned early to let my clubs do the talking, as my mom had always advised me. She taught me to be strong, and that the more I said, the worse the situation would be. If I was going to let my clubs do the talking, Mom said, I might as well beat the other guys by as many shots as I could.

There was a difference between winning and beating. I wanted to win, sure, but I also wanted to win by as many shots as possible. My mom liked me to "stomp" on the other players, to use her word. I started to become what my dad called an "assassin" on the course. I developed that attitude at an early age, without intending to. It was just who I was. The more pressure there was in a tournament, the more I had to make a shot to keep a match going, or to win a match or a tournament, the calmer I felt. As I started to play more tournaments and make my way in junior golf, I thirsted for that moment. I'm sure Nicklaus did as well. He wanted the shot when it mattered most.

Tom Weiskopf once said something very revealing about Nicklaus's state of mind. Jack was coming up the final hole of a tournament when Tom said, "Jack has the presence of mind to make the right decision when all around him players are getting confused and panicky." Jack was calmer and more locked in the more a tournament was on the line. I'm not sure that can be taught, but I do know it's where you want to be when a tournament is hanging in the balance. Maybe that's intimidation. I don't know. I'm just glad I've always wanted to have to make the shot.

* * *

After watching Jack win the '86 Masters, I made sure I watched the tournament every year. Something dramatic seemed to happen year after year. In 1987 Larry Mize holed a long pitch and run from right of the eleventh green and one hundred and forty feet from the hole, to win in a play-off over Greg Norman. The ball ran and ran, pretty much on a straight line to the hole. You can't play the shot that way now, though. Augusta National raised a portion of the green there, so you have to play a different shot. The contours of Augusta's greens are complicated, which I enjoy. You could play a lot of different shots from around the greens back in 1997; you had options.

Bobby Jones and Alister MacKenzie designed Augusta National as an inland links, modeled after the Old Course at St Andrews—although they look so different from one another. A links allows the golfer to use the ground, rather than forcing only one shot—the high ball meant to fly a specific distance, land on the green, and stop within a few feet. You have to do that on most American courses, because water and sand often intervene between the player and the green. This takes away from the creativity that makes golf so much fun.

Augusta in '97 played like the inland links the designers intended. They designed it to force you to create shots around the greens. There was no rough. You had all the mounds and the options of bumping the ball. When I first played the course in the 1995 Masters, the greens and tees were close to each other, like at a links. That's not the case as much anymore, because they've lengthened so many of the holes and moved tees.

I've loved links golf since the first time I saw it

in person, when I played the 1995 Scottish Open at Carnoustie. I played the Open Championship the following week at the Old Course. Those two weeks provided a strong introduction to links golf. I made the cut at both tournaments, although my finishes were poor; I was forty-seventh in the Scottish and sixty-eighth in the Open. But it was more important that I'd discovered links golf, and that I could see the relationship between the type of golf you wanted to play there and the type you wanted to play at Augusta, especially if Augusta was firm during the Masters so that you could use the slopes in the fairways and on the greens.

At the 1995 Masters—months before I'd play the Scottish Open at Carnoustie—I often had the option of creating shots on the ground, to play links-like golf on an inland course. The only difference was that I was playing on bent grass and the greens were running at thirteen on the Stimpmeter, that device where a ball is placed on an inclined plane and allowed to roll down to the green. If the ball rolled out to thirteen feet, then the Stimp measurement was said to be thirteen. Bent running at thirteen on the Stimp was different from the fescue or meadow grasses on a links, where the greens couldn't be as fast in case it got very windy.

Strategic golf appealed to me, although I enjoyed

and even thrived in amateur golf on the excitement that came when I was required to hit one shot and one shot only over water, and you'd better do it now, as Jack had to do on that fifteenth hole on the last day of the 1986 Masters. I just never wanted that kind of golf as a steady diet. I found too much of it boring. It didn't ask a golfer to imagine and create shots. It didn't generate confusion in a player's mind. There was one choice: the air ball.

The golf on the ground that Augusta offered, especially into and around the greens, appealed to me even when I was a kid. I'm not sure why, because I grew up playing a lot of courses where the idea was to fly the ball all the way to the hole—the air game. But I enjoyed the creativity you could put into shots on the ground—the shots you could invent. Also, Augusta gave you a chance if you weren't in a good situation. It gave you an opportunity to bail out. But if you did bail out, you'd have one of the hardest pitches on the planet. Mize's shot was a good example of that. Nicklaus's four-iron to the fifteenth hole in '86, on the other hand, was the perfect example of golf in the air. Augusta National demanded both.

Every year when I was a kid watching the Masters telecast, I got more excited about the possibility of my playing the tournament one day. Even though some members had invited me, I didn't want to play the course until I qualified for the tournament. I didn't want to go until I'd earned my way in. Then, nine years after watching Jack win that 1986 Masters, I was about to get my chance. I qualified for the 1995 Masters because I'd won the U.S. Amateur the year before. I was nineteen, and nobody would have referred to me as sentimental about golf. I'd developed a respect for the course and the Masters, but I would never refer to it as a "cathedral in the pines"—the term you hear every April. I did enjoy reading golf history, and I had studied the Masters. But I didn't think the history of the place would overwhelm me. I wanted to get there to compete. Finally, that moment arrived.

My introduction to Augusta National came when I entered the club from Washington Road—the main street running through the city—and came to Magnolia Lane. I don't know what I expected, but I was underwhelmed. It was a quick drive of about three hundred yards, framed by magnolia trees whose branches hung over the road. I was surprised by how short the drive was, only about the length of the range that we used then. I'd thought from watching the tournament on television that Magnolia Lane was much longer, and that it went up a hill to the clubhouse. Or maybe I was underwhelmed because the club had excluded black golfers from playing for so long. Twenty years had passed since Lee Elder became the first African-American to be invited to play the Masters. That was forty-one years since the first Masters, and Charlie Sifford, for one, ought to have been invited because he had won on the PGA Tour, but he never was. My dad said a couple of days later that Magnolia Lane didn't impress a black golfer because of this history. I'd grown up hearing about the history along with learning that the Masters was the most popular tournament in the world. I had wanted to compete in the Masters ever since I got serious about golf. All of this was probably playing on my mind as we drove down Magnolia Lane. I had complicated feelings, but most of all, I was eager to get to the clubhouse and onto the course for my first round at Augusta National.

It was Sunday evening, about seven. I'd driven to Augusta National with my Stanford teammate and close friend Notah Begay, after we played a couple of college tournaments in Atlanta and Dalton, Georgia. Nobody was at the club except for the receptionist. She showed me up to my room in the Crow's Nest. I settled in, then went to the practice green with Notah. He wasn't playing in the Masters, but it was good to have a pal with me. We hit some putts and then went back in the clubhouse to get something to eat. I got lost finding my way back and ended up in the Champions locker room after using the wrong door. That was my first experience of the Champions room. I looked in and saw all the lockers: Sam Snead, Jack Nicklaus, Arnold Palmer, Billy Casper, and Gene Sarazen—all the Masters champions. I had read about these champions and been impressed, but seeing their names on the lockers made an immediate and deep impression on me. I yearned to get my name on a locker. Of course I wasn't even allowed in there, because I hadn't earned my way in. I'd have to win the Masters to be there legitimately.

I returned to the Crow's Nest, which felt like a frat house to me during my stay. It's all single beds, and open, with little dividers. There was one phone to share, so everybody could hear whatever conversations you were having. I didn't have a cellphone then. Hardly anybody did, and certainly none of us in the Crow's Nest had one. I was sharing the Crow's Nest with Trip Kuehne, Tim Jackson, Guy Yamamoto, and Lee James. Trip was the '94 U.S. Amateur finalist, and the guy I beat to win the Am. We both qualified for the Masters off those finishes. Tim was the U.S. Mid-Amateur champion, Guy had won the U.S. Public Links, and Lee had won the '94 British Amateur. Trip and Lee were twenty-two, Guy was in his midthirties, and Tim in his late thirties.

After an unusually long night's sleep Sunday, I got up and was ready to play Augusta National—well, maybe not quite ready in the sense of being prepared—but I was eager to get on the course. I'd also watched previous Masters that my parents had taped, and, at Stanford, I practiced putting at Maples Pavilion on the hardwood floor of the volleyball court. I showed up there, putter in hand. That got a lot of laughs, but I didn't care. I hit a lot of forty-foot putts, just touching the ball, trying to put a soft stroke on it. One thing was certain. I didn't want to tighten my grip and lose any feel.

I played my first practice round with Lee James and Nick Faldo, who had won in 1989 and 1990 and who had more control of the ball than anybody at the time. He was a precision player. My father walked along, and so did Ron Townsend and Bill Simms. They were the first two black members at Augusta National. Townsend, then the president of the Gannett Television Group, was invited to join in 1990, while Simms, who owned a 5 percent stake in the Carolina Panthers, became a member four years later.

Tommy Bennett, a local guy and a veteran caddie, was on my bag. His nickname was Burnt Biscuits. Ward Clayton, in his book about Augusta's caddies, wrote that Tommy turned over a pot of boiling water that was on the stove as he tried to escape out the kitchen window from his grand-mother's home with some biscuits. But he burned his legs with the hot water. He was popular enough around Augusta that there was a fading mural of him on the front brick wall of the Sand Hill Grill; it showed him wearing the Augusta National white overalls and a green Masters cap. I visited the Grill during the week to get some local knowledge from the caddies, for whom it was a hangout. He carried my black leather bag with some gold stitching, from the 1994 World Amateur Team Championships in Versailles, which the United States won.

Out on the course, Faldo was intense, and while I might have liked to question him about his strat-egy as we played, it was apparent that he wanted to mostly keep to himself. That was okay with me. I was the kid. He was the veteran and two-time Mas-ters champion who went on to win a third Masters in 1996. Lee and I were more talkative because we were contemporaries. He was three years older than I was, but he was also playing in his first Masters, and we were both staying in the Crow's Nest. We enjoyed the round and went our separate ways. I wasn't prepared for what happened next.

The media were waiting under the massive oak tree on the lawn at the back of the clubhouse that serves as a gathering place for media, players, and Masters visitors who have access there. I passed it on my way to the clubhouse, as all players did. They stopped if anybody wanted to interview them. I made the mistake of walking right past the media, because I had decided I didn't want to be distracted. Besides, I was going to do a press conference on Tuesday. It didn't occur to me that I would need to speak with the media after my first practice round. I thought I had a decent relationship with the media coming into the Masters. I'd spent time with them while winning amateur tournaments and had become accustomed to mass press conferences. The first one I did was when I was sixteen at the LA Open. Why couldn't the media wait until the Tuesday press conference at Augusta? But I was wrong. I should have stopped.

I'd won three straight U.S. Juniors, and then the '94 U.S. Amateur, and the media had started to take a lot of interest. I soon realized that print, radio, and television journalists were going to want to talk to me after every round, during practice or the tournament, and no matter what I shot. Rookie mistake, I guess. I went inside the clubhouse and had lunch with Trip. He and I had played one another in the final match of the 1994 U.S. Amateur, at the TPC Stadium course at Sawgrass. I was 6 down to Trip after thirteen holes in the morning and 3 down with nine holes to play in the afternoon round. But I came back to win my first U.S. Amateur. I went out with Trip for a second practice round Monday at Augusta. We played a five-dollar match, and I nipped him on the last hole to win.

My Tuesday practice round was with Greg Norman, Fred Couples, and Ray Floyd. Freddie and Raymond were former Masters champions. I wanted to learn from the guys who not only knew the course but who had won, or come close, as Norman had. I asked questions nonstop. *What do you do here, what do you do there?* I'm sure they got tired of me. But this was history. I had the chance to tap into history. Why wouldn't I ask?

The pin was on the right side of the second green, and I wanted to know the best way to get to it. Raymond said, "See those people over there?" He was pointing to the people right of the green. He told me to hit my second right at them. I said, "What? You don't try to funnel it in off the slope? You don't go for the green on your second shot after a good drive?" Raymond was showing me what he would sometimes do. He was shorter than I was off the tee. The two bunkers on the right didn't exist for me. But Raymond played left of them. He wanted to show me an unusual route to give myself the best chance for birdie if I did happen to drive it short one day and couldn't get to the green with my second shot. Raymond said, "Just hit it over to the right or hit it into the people, or hit it into number three in front of the tee, and then pitch back up."

I asked, "Why would you do that?"

He told me to go down there to have a look. I walked over, asked some of the spectators to move, and threw a few balls down. From there I could see exactly why Raymond intentionally hit his second so far right sometimes. He had the entire green to work with on his third shot, and was pitching into it uphill. The ball wouldn't run out because of that. You weren't at the mercy of the hill.

I pitched back up the hill, and I saw, yeah, this is a pretty easy shot, even to a left flag. Okay, cool. So I said, "It's nice, it's really nice down there, and the angle is good to pitch up the hill." The way Raymond played the second shot didn't compute for me unless for some reason I couldn't get to the green, but the idea made sense. Augusta lengthened the hole a few years later, and I did try the shot he suggested. I would never have seen that shot if he hadn't pointed it out to me. That was the advantage of practicing with guys who had a lot of experience at Augusta. It was good of them to play with me and to show me around. There's a reason only one golfer,

Fuzzy Zoeller, has won the Masters in his first time there in modern times. It takes time to understand the nuances of the course.

Raymond taught me a few other little shots around Augusta, different cuts and spins. We were using the old balata ball, which made those types of shots easier. I learned how the guys would hook little chips, and cut 'em, how to kill the speed into this slope, to use that slope. Essentially I learned about the different shots and clubs they used, and the options that they had. There were so many more options around the greens back then. Augusta has changed dramatically since those days, when we used a ball with much more spin, and there were much tighter conditions around the greens. You had more shots. These guys knew them all.

That Tuesday, I did my press conference. I said that I was trying to treat the Masters like any other tournament. My thinking was that the game was the same as in college golf or any other pro event, even if the spotlight was so much brighter on the Masters than the tournaments I'd played while I was at Stanford. I didn't mean to offend anybody. I was being honest, but I learned that I had offended some of the media, and I got ripped. The Masters was a major, and the first one every year. When I was asked whether I was thrilled to be at Augusta,

I said yes, I was thrilled, but my primary focus was on my game and not the atmosphere. That didn't go over too well. My deal was that I entered every tournament, no matter what it was, to win. I wasn't about to get distracted and overwhelmed by a place or its history. I had read about the Masters and knew plenty about its history. I felt I could talk about it with anybody, and I'd be glad to do that—but after the tournament. I wanted to focus only on my game and the shots I needed to play. I felt that way at every tournament. The Masters was no different. That was just the way I felt.

I was being honest, but I sensed a tense atmosphere in the media center. When I was asked why golfers seemed to know more about the history of our sport than other athletes did of theirs, I answered, "Why? Hell if I know. I honestly can't answer that because I really don't know. Why do we?" My answers to some of the questions weren't going over well. I was also asked what I thought about the fact that I was only the fourth black to play in the Masters—after Lee Elder in 1975, followed by Jim Thorpe and Cal Peete. "Have you encountered any problems?" a reporter asked. I answered, "I have not encountered any problem except for the speed of the greens."

I was well aware of Augusta's history before 1975 of not inviting players whose accomplishments should have gotten them in, and also of the club's history, until 1990, of not inviting a black person to join. But I refused to get drawn into a discussion of these matters during the press conference. Still, my awareness of the club's history had something to do with my not feeling blown away by Magnolia Lane and being there. I did feel a bit like a fish out of water—I was not a country club kid—as much as I enjoyed reading about the Masters.

One more day of practice remained. Greg asked if I'd like to play again with him, which I appreciated. Nick Price joined us. Nick hadn't won the Masters, but he had won the 1992 and 1994 PGA Championships, and the 1994 British Open. He finished '94 as the number one ranked player in the world. I looked forward to my first round with Nick, and to checking out in person his brisk swing and manner. It was better to play quickly than slowly; you'd be likely to have fewer swing thoughts and to have a clear mind when you took the club back. Nick made quick decisions and locked into his target. It also was encouraging to know that Nick had shot 63 in the 1986 Masters. Greg would shoot 63 in the 1996 Masters. That's the course record to this day.

I later played with Nick during the 1995 U.S. Open at Shinnecock Hills Golf Club on Long Island when he shot 66 in the opening round—I shot 74.

Afterward, I asked Nick in the locker room how many pins he had gone for. He said he didn't go for more than a couple, and asked me how many I had tried to get to. "Every one," I said. He had given me a hell of a lesson right there. You could go low while playing conservative, smart golf in a major. I've never forgotten that lesson.

Nick, Greg, and I had a good time, and I continued to learn when to be aggressive on the course, when to go at some holes depending on where the flags were on the greens, and when to play away from them. We talked a lot, but, unfortunately, my lesson with Nick and Greg lasted only five holes. I felt a twinge in my back on the fifth tee, and returned to the clubhouse after I hit my second shot. Frank Jobe, the orthopedic surgeon who had pioneered the surgery that saved the career of Los Angeles Dodgers pitcher Tommy John—the surgery, to repair a torn elbow ligament, became known as Tommy John surgery—was on-site. He had also pioneered the availability of a fitness trailer on the PGA Tour. Dr. Jobe checked me out and concluded I had suffered a sprain and from that a muscle spasm. The PGA Tour's physical therapist, Ralph Sampson, was also on-site. He worked on me for ninety minutes until he decided it was okay for me to hit balls.

I was already getting used to injuries, having had

my first knee surgery back at school. I wished it wasn't that way, but there wasn't much I could do but be mentally tough enough to cope with any pain and to play through it. I hit some short irons and then played the Par 3 Contest in the afternoon with Gary Player and Tim Jackson. Playing with Gary provided another learning experience for me. I'd already had quite a Masters, having played with some of the best players in the game.

That Wednesday night I got my typical five hours of sleep, and then ran in the morning. I was going to play with Ollie. He'd won the 1994 Masters, so as the 1994 U.S. Amateur champion I would be playing the first round with him. I looked forward not only to my first round competing in the Masters but to playing with Ollie.

My practice rounds had confirmed to me what I had hoped I would see: that Augusta National was perfect for me. I was hitting it farther than most of the guys were hitting it. If I drove it halfway decent, I'd be able to reach all the par-5s and probably have eight or nine wedges into the par-4s. That makes golf a lot easier.

A light, misty rain was falling as we teed off. Tommy Bennett had already caddied in fifteen Masters, and so it made sense for me to have such an experienced caddie in my first Masters. What did I know about the course? I knew what I'd seen on television and heard from guys who had played the course. But the only sure way of truly appreciating what I needed to do was to get out there. I'd thought that my dad might caddie for me, because nobody knew me better. But he was sixty-two, and Augusta is a hilly course. We decided it would be smarter for me to work with Tommy.

I was extremely nervous on the first tee. My heart and my mind were racing, and I didn't know what kind of swing I'd make. Butchie and I always made sure that I hit my last shot on the range the way I wanted to hit my opening drive. We then headed over to the first tee, and I heard that little voice in my head telling me to trust my swing. I swung as hard as I could and hit the ball as hard as I could to keep it between the trees on either side of the fairway. I bombed it over the top of the bunker and had only a sand wedge in. I should have gone more at the flag and put it underneath the hole to where I was putting along the ridge there. But I chickened out and hit the shot pin-high in the center of the green. That wasn't very good, with a sand wedge in my hand. I had about a twenty-five-footer, and I hit what I didn't think was too bad a putt. I'd hit it a bit hard, but no big deal. It kept trickling, and kept going, right to left and past the hole, and then it kept going, and ended up catching the ridge. People on the other side of the green started moving. It's never good when you hit a putt and people start to move.

My next shot was one of the hardest golf shots on the planet. It was muddy and wet, and I was in the gallery playing my third shot after hitting the green with my second. I had to play a bump spinner, driving it into the hill, and to make sure I got the ball on top of the ridge. I also had to spin it if I wanted to get it close. But I went for the chicken way again and put the ball back on the same line from where I'd putted off the green. I had ten feet for bogey, and at least I knew the speed of the putt. I made it. Great start to my Augusta career. Hit the green in regulation, and then hit my first putt off the green.

Walking to the second tee, I told myself to pound it over the bunker on the right, and I did. I had a cocky walk off that tee, because I'd done what I wanted to do. Ollie was saying, "What the hell is this kid doing?" He didn't think there was any way somebody could carry the top of that bunker. Ollie wasn't ever the longest hitter, and he was still using persimmon woods. I was using a Tour Burner Plus driver from TaylorMade, and had a big advantage because I could carry the ball 280 yards. That was a big carry at the time. I hit six-iron to the green and made 4, so I was back to even par. Ollie said I was hitting the ball so far that he needed binoculars to see it.

I'd gotten off to a decent start, and I saw my name on the leaderboard. I'd never seen my name on a leaderboard in a tour event before. I saw all my numbers, hole by hole, and my name. There it was: WOODS. It was the coolest thing ever. I took that feeling in, and then refocused that energy onto my next shot. I shot 72 that opening round, and 72 the next round. Coming up the eighteenth fairway to the green in the second round, knowing I would make the cut, I saw my father and mother and Jay Brunza (my friend, sometimes caddie, and a naval psychologist, primarily working with kids going through chemotherapy). Jay lived in San Diego and had driven up to Cypress every Saturday to join me and some other good players in games at the Navy course. He had helped me with my mental game and had caddied for me in some big national tournaments.

Seeing them meant a lot to me. Here I was, nearing the end of my second round at Augusta, and I'd made it to the weekend—the only one of the five amateurs to do that. I'd not made it to the weekend in any of the seven PGA Tour events I'd played until then. I think I lost some focus then, though. I three-putted the last green. I wasn't happy, but then again, 72-72 was a decent way to start my first Masters. I had a lot to learn, and my first two rounds in the Masters helped me feel I was doing all the right things to develop my game.

But maybe not. I turned it around real quick in the third round—the wrong way—and shot 77. That time I was distracted. The lesson was obvious: I needed to be relentless in my determination to stay focused. They took my name off real quick. I decided to change my irons for the last round. I borrowed a set from Butchie and birdied three of the last four holes, including the eighteenth. The 72 put me at 293—5 over par and in a tie for forty-first place.

The next morning I had a nine a.m. history class at Stanford, so I had to get out that night. But first I left a letter for Augusta National:

Please accept my sincere thanks for providing me the opportunity to experience the most wonderful week of my life. It was fantasyland and Disney World wrapped into one. I was treated like a gentleman throughout my stay and I trust I responded in kind. The Crow's Nest will always remain in my heart and your magnificent golf course will provide a continuing challenge throughout my amateur and professional career.

I've accomplished much here and learned even more. Your tournament will always hold a special spot in my heart as the place where I made my first PGA cut and at a major yet! It is here that I left my youth behind and became a man. For that I will be eternally in your debt. With warmest regards and deepest appreciation.

Sincerely,
Tiger Woods

I flew home that Sunday night, from Augusta to Atlanta to San Francisco. At nine a.m. Monday, I was in my history class at Stanford.

But soon there was trouble at Stanford, and not in history class. During the tournament, I had written a diary, which was published in *Golf World* and *Golfweek* magazines—an unpaid activity, of course. Writing for payment was a potential violation of my amateur and NCAA status, something Stanford had to take seriously. Steve Mallonee, the director of legislative services for the NCAA, said that my writing for the magazines, even though I wasn't paid, was "deemed to be a promotion of a commercial publication," and that Stanford's investigation was "in accordance with the rules." I was subsequently suspended for a day, but the decision in the end was that I'd inadvertently violated the rules, and my eligibility was restored.

None of this spoiled my first Masters for me. I kept thinking how much I'd learned from my practice rounds and the guys I played with, and from the tournament itself. I needed to sharpen my iron game. My distance control wasn't where it needed to be. I went all out on my shots into the greens, usually hitting the ball as hard as I could. I didn't have the off-speed swing that was sometimes called for, and I also spun the ball too much because I hit it so hard.

I'd been working with Butchie since after the 1993 U.S. Amateur, when I lost in the second round at the Champions Golf Club in Houston. My dad contacted Butchie at the Lochinvar Country Club, where he was the head pro, and asked if he would consider working with me. Butchie agreed and said it would take three years for me to refine my game and get it to where I should be able to contend in every tournament I played. We had worked on flattening the plane of my swing and on shortening my backswing. After my first Masters, I understood I needed to swing at less than full speed, hit the ball down when I wanted to, and be able to take spin off some shots, as required.

* * *

While working with Butchie after the '95 Masters, I started to get more comfortable hitting off-speed shots. My dad watched me hit balls on the range at Carnoustie when I played the Scottish Open a few months later. I used a bunch of different clubs to hit a target two hundred yards away. He said that he hadn't seen me *play* like that in a long time. I was having fun, and using my imagination. In some ways, nothing had changed since I was a kid at the Navy course. My favorite thing was to work on my game and learn to play different shots. I got into a flow, letting myself feel shots and then going ahead and manufacturing them.

Five years later, during the Open Championship at the Old Course, David Duval and I were the only ones out on the practice range as night approached. The fans sitting in stands were asking us to have some fun, maybe put on a trick show of sorts. David and I said, sure, what the heck. We hit shots simultaneously. I'd hit a hook, and David would hit a slice, or vice versa. The balls crisscrossed in flight.

We were a couple of golfers enjoying ourselves as we would on our own—having some fun and entertaining the spectators. It didn't matter that we were doing it during a major. The more I thought about it, though, the more it made sense to have some fun like that at a major. You think you need to do something different because you're playing a major. But you don't need to do anything more than play smart.

I shot 69-71 to make the cut in the 1995 Scottish Open at Carnoustie, but closed with 75-78. In the Open at the Old Course, I shot 74-71-72-78. I thoroughly enjoyed the nuances of the course and the options around the greens. Playing links golf enabled me to indulge my creativity on the course. The Old Course, like Augusta National, has a lot of nuances that take time to appreciate. My finishes weren't what I'd hoped for, but I felt myself maturing as a golfer.

Next up was the 1995 U.S. Amateur, at the Newport Country Club in Newport, Rhode Island. I qualified for match play, although I didn't play very well. Still, I was in the championship, and had the opportunity to win my second straight U.S. Amateur and fifth straight USGA championship. (I had won those '91, '92, and '93 U.S. Juniors.) Jay Brunza had caddied for me in those four national championships, and he was on my bag again in Newport. The course was dry, hard, and fast. It was on the East Coast by the ocean, and it felt linksy to me.

I reached the finals and then came to the last hole of the thirty-six-hole match 1 up over Buddy Marucci, a forty-three-year-old career amateur who belonged to Pine Valley, Seminole, and Merion—three of the best courses in the United States, and another golf world from the one where I'd grown up in Cypress. He hit his second shot to the eighteenth green to about twenty feet from the hole. I had 140 yards to the hole. The green was elevated, and I figured I could hit a stock nine-iron. But I'd need to hit it hard to get it there, and I didn't want to do that because of the spin I'd impart to the ball. Instead, I chose an eight-iron and decided to take some speed and spin off the shot—more or less a dead-hands shot. Butchie and I had drilled on this shot since the Masters. I put it into play.

The shot came off exactly as I wanted, landing fifteen feet behind the hole and then spinning back down a slope—but not spinning too much. It finished a foot and a half from the hole. Buddy missed his birdie putt and conceded my putt. I had taken my second straight U.S. Amateur. Butchie was thrilled, as I was. He said I couldn't have hit that eight-iron four months before, when I'd played my first Masters. The win got me into the '96 Masters, and also the U.S. and British Opens that year.

I wrote to Arnold Palmer well in advance of the Masters to ask if he would play a practice round with me. He agreed to do that on Wednesday morning. In the end, I played with both Arnold and Jack then. Jack and I had never played together, so now I was going to tee it up with Jack, who had won six Masters, and Arnold, who had won four. I had learned from the Masters champions I played practice rounds with in '95, and now I was sure I'd learn more. The learning curve was pretty steep.

On the first tee, Jack and Arnold said, "Let's play skins." I didn't have any money on me, so I was thinking, please don't say a number that's high, or any number at all. We played for a nominal amount. The skins is a game where the player with the low score on the hole wins the stake; if two players tie, the stakes accrue to the next hole, and so on. The stakes in our game had accrued so that it all came down to the eighteenth hole. Whoever won eighteen would win the skins.

I was grinding like hell to make birdie so that I could take their cash. How awesome would that be? I made par, and Jack made par. Arnold had a ten-footer to win the skins, and he rammed it in. He gave us a look, typical Arnold. I thanked Jack and Arnold for having me around for eighteen holes. They asked if I planned to play the Par 3 Contest that afternoon, and I said that I did. They said I should come with them, but I didn't know what they meant. They wanted me to join them in the Par 3, for another nine holes together, and that we would keep the skins going. "Really?" I asked. We didn't have a starting time. Arnold said not to worry about it.

We walked over to the first tee on the Par 3 course. Magically, we were on deck as soon as Jack and Arnold showed up. I was on the little putting green beside the tee. The green had two holes cut in it, and I was hitting a few putts. All of a sudden, we were teeing off. The best part of the nine holes was that each of us made 2 on the ninth hole. Jack won the skins, but he didn't ask me to pay. I was thankful for that.

Jack did his press conference after we played. He was asked his impressions of me. That was when he said that he and Arnold agreed I could win more Masters than the two of them combined. That would be eleven times. It was very encouraging to know that two of the best players ever—well, Jack *was* the best if you count major championship wins as the ultimate criterion—felt that way about me.

But I wasn't going to win my first Masters that year. I played with Ben Crenshaw, the defending champion, in the first round, and the only thing I did well was drive the ball long and in the fairways. I hit every fairway and ten greens, but I putted lousy. I couldn't get the speed of the greens down, and I also hit some poor short irons. My work on controlling my distance was ongoing, but I didn't show what I had at the U.S. Amateur the previous summer. I hit wedges over the green on the eleventh and fourteenth holes, and bogeyed both. I also had my issues with longer irons. I had 221 yards to the green on the second hole after busting my drive over the bunker, and then I hit a four-iron thirty yards over the green. It took me four more shots to get down. It added up to 75 for the first round. The next day was more of the same: another 75 to miss the cut by four shots. Jack was right about one thing. He'd said I might not be ready to win the Masters in only my second try. No golfer is a machine, no matter how hard we've worked. I was working on the right things, but I didn't have it in the '96 Masters. I flew back to San Francisco.

Greg Norman took a six-shot lead over Faldo into the final round. Everybody assumed he would finally win the Masters. He had come close a bunch of times, including in 1986 when he had to par the last hole to get into a play-off with Nicklaus, who had finished. He had birdied the fourteenth through the seventeenth holes and was obviously on his game. But after hitting three-wood into the eighteenth fairway, Greg pushed his four-iron way right into the gallery. He played a bump and run from there and left himself a putt of about fifteen feet. But he missed the putt. Masters chance gone.

Now, ten years later, Norman looked certain to win the Masters. But he lost the six-shot lead when he shot 78 while Faldo was shooting 67 to win. Faldo never short-sided himself during the last round. He kept the ball underneath the hole. You had to do those things to score well at Augusta, but what really struck me was how a big lead could disappear in a minute.

That Sunday, we played a qualifying tournament back home for the next Stanford tournament. Every player had to requalify in a one-day event like that to get on the team for the next tournament. If I had made the cut at the Masters, I doubt I'd have been on the team. We were playing while the final round was on at Augusta, and it wasn't until we finished that we found out what had happened. I felt for Norman, but it was another important lesson to learn. I kept it in mind a year later. It was possible to come back from a bad start, as I'd do after shooting 40 that front nine in the 1997 Masters, and it was also possible to blow a big lead the last day. Even a very big lead.

Chapter Three

Monday, April 7, 1997

This was what I'd been waiting for since I turned professional nearly eight months before: my first Masters as a professional. I'd been practicing for this moment since the start of the year, even during other tournaments where I had worked on shots that I knew I would need at the Masters: hitting the ball high, with a slight draw; getting my lag putting down so that I would have as many tap-ins as possible for my second putt. Butchie and I were pointing to the Masters; we were pointing hard.

Because my preferred shot at Augusta was a right-to-left shot, I felt one way to encourage that in practice was to hit balls with a persimmon-headed driver. I had an old Cleveland Classic driver and an old MacGregor Eye-O-Matic driver, and I used them to ensure I was hitting the ball in the right spot to promote a draw. The idea was to use the gear effect that you could get then with persimmon. The heads were small enough compared with the size they would become, and they had enough bulge and roll so that if I made a normal swing intending to hit the ball off the toe, the ball would draw. If I hit it toward the heel, the ball faded. I could shape the ball any way I wanted. If I aimed down the left side of the fairway and hit it off the heel, the ball always peeled back to the right. Off the toe, draw. There's no gear effect now with the enormous, titanium drivers in play. Hit it off the heel, and the ball keeps going left. Hit it off the toe, it keeps going right. I felt I could feel the face on the ball more when I practiced with persimmon; the clubs became ideal training tools for me as I prepared for Augusta.

Every new calendar year, the Masters felt to me as though it was just around the corner; it was on my mind all the time and I felt I had to begin to prepare. I did the same thing when I was younger for the Junior World, the U.S. Junior, and then the U.S. Amateur; after I turned pro, I'd start thinking about the four majors. Above all tournaments, I wanted to peak for those.

It was obvious to me when I'd played Augusta National as an amateur that I'd need to hit the ball as high as possible to carry some of the bunkers, mounds, and hills off the tees. So my objective during practice sessions and casual rounds for the Masters was not only to flight the ball right to left, but also to get comfortable hitting the ball high. I was using the same yardage book as in 1995 and 1996 during practice, because the course had hardly changed. The changes were to come later, after the club decided it had to lengthen the course and make other modifications to counteract how far players were hitting the ball.

Fluff and I had the carry distances to the mounds on the fifteenth hole; we had stepped them off, and they were my targets. The mounds would kick a drive that landed in the area forward and get the ball running fast. We also had important carry yardages on other holes. Butchie and I talked during practice leading up to the Masters about shots I needed to hit on the holes. He would say, "Okay, you're on the fifteenth tee. Drive it so that you'll carry the mounds on the right side." If I hit my spots on the par-5s, I would hit the speed slots and come into them with middle to short irons, and into the par-4s with wedges. I would effectively turn the par-5s into par-4s.

As I learned about playing Augusta National, it became apparent to me that it was important to hit the ball high to carry the bunkers around the greens. That was the only way to get close to some of the pin positions. There was no point, then, in working on hitting the ball low going into Augusta. It wasn't surprising to me that Lee Trevino never figured he had a good chance of winning the Masters. He had great control over the ball, but he was a low-ball hitter. His best finishes at the Masters were in 1975 and 1985, when he tied for tenth. He won two U.S. Opens, two British Opens, and two PGA Championships. But the Masters eluded him. The course didn't suit him, as creative a shotmaker as he was. Trevino said so, especially when he decided not to play the 1970, 1971, and 1974 Masters. Later, I heard the real reason he didn't play those years was because he didn't get along with Clifford Roberts, the club founder and tournament chairman, from the first day they met, and that he was actually fine with the course. I'm not sure what the truth is, but I was aware that Augusta was a place of legends that were both positive and negative.

I'd also heard the rumbles about black golfers not being welcome at the Masters. Everybody was writing about me as an African-American who was playing in his first Masters as a professional. I tried to make it clear that I was African-American on my dad's side and Asian on my mom's side, and that to think of me only as an African-American was to deny my mom's heritage. At the 1995 U.S. Open, I had referred to myself as a Cablinasian, a made-up word that includes my Caucasian, black, and Asian heritage. I never thought it was right or fair to think of me only as an African-American, and I never will. But I had learned that to have one drop of black blood in you in America meant that you were considered an African-American.

I was focused on being a golfer, and I wished people could see me as only a golfer, but clearly that wasn't going to happen. Nevertheless I could still control my golf game. The way for me to give myself the best chance of winning was to hit the ball high, leave myself in the right spots coming into the greens, and control the speed of my putts. That's what I had been focused on.

I put in a lot of time on all parts of my game—except for the low ball. I'd been working with Butchie since the start of the year on getting less aggressive with my putting. As a junior and then as an amateur, I tended to pretty much go for every putt, which would often leave me with too much work to do when my first putt went well by the hole. But that was my nature. I was all-out on every part of my game, and I carried this attitude right through the bag, driver to putter. At both Bay Hill and the Players Championship, a couple of weeks before the

Masters, Butchie and I both felt that I started to get the feel of what *cup speed* meant. I learned how to hit a putt so that it could go in from any part of the hole, front, back, sides, and all points in between. As for my swing, I'd continued to work on taking spin off my irons, so that the ball wouldn't spin back when it hit the greens at Augusta.

I was the kind of golfer who liked to be more aggressive than conservative in my shots, without taking on ridiculous risks when the penalty for a missed shot was extreme. Still, it wasn't easy for me to curb my go-for-it nature. Augusta's greens demanded a more cautious approach. A sure way out of the tournament would be to constantly face comeback putts for par after running the ball a few feet past the hole on the slippery, undulating greens. I gripped the putter tightly, maybe to feel like I was stoked to make a putt. But it was dangerous to putt like that at Augusta. Butchie came up with a novel way to help me go easier on the putter, and to grip it, if not more softly, then at least without what golfers call a "death" grip. Butchie found a manufacturer that made a putter that would beep if I squeezed the grip tightly. Put the pressure on it, and I got the beep. I hated the thing, but it was useful. I practiced with it at home and in hotel rooms during tournaments. But there was no way I would take it to the tournament, even during practice rounds. I'd feel embarrassed if the thing beeped, and I often had trouble stopping it from beeping.

You would think I could just tell myself to ease up on the grip, but I found it difficult. I could take a light grip over the ball, but then I would instinctively squeeze the grip as I made my forward press just before taking the putter back. Butchie laughed as only he can when I couldn't stop myself from taking a tight grip, but I eventually learned to ease up. Still, it's always been a tendency of mine to grab the grip and give it a squeeze.

Meanwhile, I spent countless hours working on other parts of my short game, too. I was lucky that I'd spent some time with Seve Ballesteros in Houston when we were both working with Butchie. Seve had won the Masters in 1980 and 1983. I'd watched the tournaments on videotape. You often heard the word *magician* applied to Seve when it came to his short game, and that was what he was: a magician. I got to thinking he could do almost anything with the ball around the greens. He spent hours showing me his short game. We played until dark. I wanted to see how he did it. I wasn't able to play all of the shots he had, but I could take pieces. I asked him how he did it, but knowing how didn't mean I could, which was fine because I didn't need to have all his shots, or to play them as he would. I could be creative in my own way.

Marko had also helped me prepare for Augusta, as I worked toward getting into what my dad called "major mode." Even though I'd played the Masters twice, I was still young and raw. While playing with Marko at Isleworth, I had seen that I really didn't know how to play the game. I could hit it for miles, but that was the easy part. I needed a wider variety of shots, and I hadn't yet developed the physical parts of the game. My game was relatively immature—all power with whatever club I had in my hands.

Butchie asked me during our first session together after the '93 Amateur if I had a go-to, automatic shot when I wasn't swinging well. Every golfer needs a reliable shot that he can put in play, and I didn't have one. I told Butchie that my go-to shot was what I did just about every time: swing as fast as I could, unleashing everything I had through the ball. I then would go find the ball and hit it again. He thought I was a cocky kid, playing golf that way, and he was right. But he liked my attitude. I had my own style—just one way, sure, but it had worked, at least as far as winning. I'd won three straight U.S. Juniors by the time Butchie and I got together. Did I know how to score and how to win? Yes, at the junior level. I knew how to get the job done. But

I needed more shots, and I needed to maintain my distance while getting more accurate.

It was evident that I would have mostly short irons into the greens at Augusta. But I didn't know how to dial it down, how to hit the little half shots, or how to be proficient at hitting the ball to the yardage I wanted, whatever it was for the shot. Butchie harped at me to understand how to hit the ball pin-high. That didn't mean flag-high. *Pin-high* meant whatever you decided was your number, not necessarily where the flag was. If the flag was 164 yards, maybe I'd want to make sure my ball carried 160 yards to keep it short of the hole and leave myself an uphill putt.

There were so many holes at Augusta where I needed to learn the right spots to have my ball finish, depending on the pin position. The ninth green was an obvious example. I learned in the 1995 Masters that I should never be past the hole. I could putt off the green from there. But how do I hit my approach to a place that isn't really drawing my attention? Like all golfers, I had trouble seeing anything but the pin. By the 1997 Masters, I'd learned to focus on the number I needed to carry the ball so that it would finish in the right spot. I'd learned to keep the pin out of my mind's eye. Marko helped me with that. It wasn't easy. It never would be easy.

I arrived in Augusta Monday after flying up from Orlando with Marko. My dad arrived the next day, with his physician, Dr. Gene McClung, who stayed at the house. My mom was there, and so were my friends Mikey Gout and Jerry Chang.

Mikey and I grew up on the same street and went to elementary school together. After school we played basketball or hung out at each other's house playing video games. There was a field between our houses, and we'd grab some clubs and hit balls there. My dad offered Mikey some lessons. But Mikey was more interested in soccer.

One day I was playing football with Mikey and a couple of other friends. I had the ball and did my usual showboating thing, running down the field and not looking ahead. I ran into a tree and was knocked out cold. The tree flexed down. I had a concussion. Like idiots, the guys didn't want to take me back home, because they were afraid of how my mom would react. The guys did, however, carry me back. Although you're supposed to wake up the guy with the concussion and observe him, my friends just dropped me off, knocked on the door, and ran. (Thanks, guys!) Despite that we've remained close friends.

Jerry and I met at Stanford. He'd been on the golf team, had just graduated, and was traveling with me. It felt like we were back in college, going from tournament to tournament, except that I was playing more tournaments and I was playing against the best players in the world. Pro golf itself, the tournament part of it, didn't feel that different from college, which was why I was glad to have my longtime pals around at the house. We had plenty of heated Ping-Pong games, and we also played video games and shot some hoops out back where the owners had a spot for that. Some of our games were pretty close, and very noisy. I felt as competitive there as on the golf course.

Jerry was the driver for the week at Augusta. He drove me to the course and back every day in the big Cadillac courtesy car that the Masters provided. And sometimes, when my dad was up to going, he would drive him, too. He usually stayed around the house when my dad was there, so that he could help him with whatever he needed. Jenny Hull, Kevin Costner's personal assistant, was also staying in the house. I'd played with Kevin at the AT&T Pebble Beach National Pro-Am earlier that year, where I met Brian Hull, his caddie and Jenny's brother. Brian played for the University of Southern California golf team. I planned to spend some time with Kevin after the Masters while he was shooting *The Postman* in Bend, Oregon.

Kathy Battaglia and Hughes Norton worked with IMG, my management agency at the time. They stayed at the IMG house, but Kathy was still the den mother for the week at our place. The house was in the Conifer neighborhood west of the course, and about ten minutes away in decent traffic. We knew that my dad wouldn't be able to get to the course every day. Kathy rented a big-screen television so that he could watch the tournament. A fellow who lived in the area cooked for us. The menu was always the same, at least for me—chicken or steak.

On Monday morning I got up at my usual time— very early. I rarely slept more than four or five hours a night and normally woke up between four and five, without an alarm clock—six was sleeping in for me. I'd used the odometer on the car to create routes in the area where we were staying of two and two and a half miles. I loved to run, and every morning I'd have my breakfast, usually some kind of oatmeal, and then get out on the streets for a four- to five-mile run out and back. My normal pace was a seven-minute mile. That was cruising. If I wanted to work hard, it was six fifteen. I'd work up a good sweat at either pace.

I'd run track in high school, and getting out by myself had been a routine of mine for a few years, including during tournaments. I felt peaceful out there in the darkness, and could let anything and everything flow through my mind. Running for me was meditative. I could run off any kind of stress, anxiety, excitement, or nervous energy. Sometimes, while running in bad weather, I'd want to stop because it was raining and cold. But I wouldn't let myself quit, and I would use the situation as motivation. Running in nasty conditions gave me an opportunity to test my will, maybe even to build it. I'd think of something Muhammad Ali said, that the will must be stronger than the skill. I wanted to see myself as an athlete and do the things that athletes do.

Many people didn't consider golf a sport. When I played on my high school golf team, I wasn't even thought of as an athlete. But I had to work out in high school. I didn't have a choice. I had to participate in the team workouts, and get in the weight room and do lifts. Then I realized this was helping me, and I began to enjoy it.

I felt golf should be and could be a sport, and that the fitter I became, the more likely I would do well. But my dad also had taught me since I was a kid to make my mind strong. I'd learned as an amateur— when I'd come from behind time after time to win national championships—and during my first seven months as a pro that my mind could be my most powerful ally. The thing was to never give up, from the first shot on the first hole to the last shot on the last hole. The first hole was as important as the last hole, and every shot was exactly the same. I had the same focus, the same intensity. I didn't try harder the deeper I got into a tournament. Nothing changed. I was busting myself as hard as I could from the first shot. I learned to have that mentality, and to maintain it. That was how I was going to approach the first shot at the Masters. Each round would take maybe five hours at the most, so I had nineteen hours to recover. Why wouldn't I focus as hard as I could for the five hours? Let's go. After that, hey, I'm done.

I needed to develop my will not only because mental strength could be such an asset in golf, but also because I'd already had some surgeries with their accompanying pain during rehab and recovery. My first surgery occurred in 1994, when I was at Stanford, with the removal of two cysts sitting on the saphenous vein on my left knee and hitting my saphenous nerve. I was left with a long scar behind my knee. The surgery was a few weeks before my nineteenth birthday on December thirtieth. I packed up my car and drove home to Cypress. I wanted to play on my birthday, so I went to rehab every day. The physios and trainers rehabbed the hell out of my knee, and finally I got the sutures out. The swelling from the bruising came down as well. I was disappointed when I was told, though, that I still wasn't ready to play. But I really wanted to tee it up. Although I had this big, old green brace on, I still asked if it would be okay if I played with it on. They wouldn't advise me to play, but they also said I wouldn't hurt myself further if I did play.

I said the heck with it, and went out to play with my dad at the Navy course. He didn't think it was a good idea. But I conned him into it. I started by asking if I could just ride in the cart with him while he played with his friends. He said, absolutely, come on. I then asked if I could bring my clubs. Maybe I could chip onto a green, or putt a little bit.

The next thing my dad knew, I was teeing it up behind the guys on the first tee. I hit it right down the middle of the fairway. Meanwhile, when they asked me how my knee felt, I'd say it was *just fine*. But in reality, the pain was excruciating and I was dying on the inside. Par for the front nine was 37. I shot 31. Then I said, "You know what, Dad? I'm done. I'll just rest it from here." I could see my skin coming out through the brace. The swelling was getting so bad that I kept strapping the brace down tighter. To me, it was like when you tweaked an ankle. You kept the shoe on. You didn't take it off, because the ankle would blow up on you. I kept it on there because I had to watch my dad and his friends play the back nine. I didn't have anyplace to go to elevate the knee and ice it. I had to ride the back nine. So I did, without letting on that I was miserable. The mind is powerful.

* * *

Jerry drove me to the course after my early-morning run. I had a question for the tournament chairman, Jack Stephens, and went to his office. "Come on over and sit right here," he said. I sat down and said, "Mr. Stephens, sir, I'm now a professional golfer, but I qualified for this tournament when I won the U.S. Amateur. It's a Masters tradition for the current U.S. Amateur champion to play the first round with the defending Masters champion, and to go off second to last. But I've been wondering whether that would still apply, since I'm here as a pro. Will I still be playing with the defending champion?"

My victories since I'd turned pro had already ensured I'd be invited to the Masters. But my eligibility off winning the U.S. Amateur wasn't in place anymore, because I had turned pro. I wasn't sure whether my winning as a pro would get me into the twosome with the defending Masters champion. I hoped it would and was eager to find out. Winning the Las Vegas Invitational, my first win as a pro, wouldn't have gotten me into the twosome with him. The defending Masters champion plays the first round with the most recent U.S. Amateur champion, not the winner of a PGA Tour event.

Mr. Stephens sat back in his chair and paused. He thought about my question. I'll never forget sitting there and waiting for his answer. He said, "Son, you've earned that right." I thanked him and told him I appreciated the opportunity. Mr. Stephens wished me good luck, and off I went. He could have answered differently. He could have said that as a pro, I wouldn't be playing with the defending champion. I'd have understood, but would have felt disappointed. Augusta National has complete control of the pairings, so they could have done whatever they chose. But Will Nicholson, Augusta's competition committee chairman then—he died in May 2016—said that when I got back into the tournament after winning as a pro, I should still play with Nick Faldo. Mr. Stephens said I earned the right to play with him. I left his office feeling really pumped.

Mr. Stephens was right. I'd earned the privilege of playing with the defending champion. It wasn't an easy decision for me to turn pro in August 1996, but I had realized, in consultation with my father, that I no longer had anything to play for in amateur golf. I'd won all the big amateur tournaments. I wanted to go to the next level.

My dad had impressed on me that I had to earn my way to the next level, and the way to do that is by winning. Eventually I went from local junior golf to national junior golf to national amateur golf. I eventually won in every age bracket growing up. But each time I moved up a bracket, I always started with a loss. I played up a bracket many times, but I got dominated at first. I wasn't good enough. Sure I could hit the ball a long way, for my age. But that didn't mean I would beat the other guys when I played up a bracket.

I was only thirteen when I lost to Justin Leonard at the Big I, the Insurance Youth Golf Classic at the Texarkana Country Club in Texarkana, Arkansas. Justin was seventeen. I hit it a long way for a thirteen-year-old, but not for a seventeen-year-old. Everybody was hitting it past me. They were young men, I was an older boy, and the difference was huge. They were simply bigger, stronger, and more efficient than I was. They knew how to control the ball. They outthought me. I had a long way to go, a long way to develop.

I finished my junior career by winning three

straight U.S. Juniors. After winning my first in July 1991, I shot 152 at the U.S. Amateur the following month to miss qualifying for the match play portion. In 1992, I shot 78-66 to qualify for match play, but lost to Tim Herron in the second round. I made it into match play again in 1993 but lost in the second round. The jump from junior golf to the next level was proving difficult for me. It was after I lost in that second round that my dad contacted Butchie and asked if he would meet me and take a look at my swing. Three years later, after I won the 1996 U.S. Amateur—my third in a row—it was apparent that I was ready to turn pro. I had successfully made the transition from junior to amateur golf, and so it was time to move on.

While the time was right, I also hadn't done much in pro tournaments that I'd played as an amateur. I'd never contended in any of the seventeen tournaments I had played. I'd made the cut in only seven of them. True, I had won the three U.S. Juniors and the three U.S. Amateurs, but that's nothing at the tour level. Now I was turning pro the week after my last U.S. Amateur, and playing in the Greater Milwaukee Open. I had seven tournaments in which I could get sponsors' exemptions and try to make enough money to earn my full playing privileges for the 1997 season. I had to earn as much as the guy who would finish 125th on the 1996 money list. I needed to play well. My mind went back to the 1992 Los Angeles Open at Riviera, where I shot 72-75 and missed the cut. I thought I did pretty well, but I was seventeen shots behind Davis Love III at that point. How could I ever make up that many shots so that I would be where he was after two rounds? I was only sixteen, but I wasn't that good. In fact, compared to the tour guys, I sucked.

It wasn't until the 1996 British Open at the Royal Lytham & St. Annes Golf Club the month before I moved on from the amateur ranks that I was finally ready to play with the pros. I made seven birdies in eleven holes in the second round, and shot 66 after opening with a 75. I shot 70-70 on the weekend for a 281 total, and was low amateur. That tied me with the English player Iain Pyman for the low amateur score in an Open; he had shot 281 in the 1993 Open at Royal St George's, which Greg Norman won.

The 66 I shot at Lytham, where I slept on the floor in the hotel because I didn't like the bed in the room—the mattress was too soft—turned things around for me, especially coming after my poor first round. It helped my confidence to know that I could make that many birdies in one round in a tour event. The seven birdies in an eleven-hole stretch came after I was 1 over for the day and 4 over for the tournament after five holes. I'm sure Richard Noon, a kid at the club and my caddie for the week, figured I was on my way to missing the cut. But years later he told Ewan Murray, a writer for the *Guardian*, that just then I said, "It's time to turn this around." Richard said that from there, "It was like a switch was flipped."

My self-confidence soared. I realized I could play this game at the pro level. I was becoming more efficient, and I wasn't wasting shots like I did when I was playing pro events earlier. I figured that I just needed to get into a rhythm of playing tour events, and then I would do well. I wasn't certain when I came to the Open that I would soon turn pro, but the second round convinced me I was good enough not only to play against tour pros, but to compete and win.

Looking back now, I do wish I had stayed one more year at Stanford, because I liked it there so much. I missed the long nights when a group of us talked about anything. I missed going away for Christmas vacation and looking forward to seeing my buddies after and catching up with them. Stanford students were exceptionally smart, so some of our discussions went far afield. One night we talked about Descartes for three hours, and our entire suite of five or six guys got deeply into it. Another night we talked about the evolution of Mongolian tribes in Central Asia. I could talk for hours about the evolution of the golf swing, but this was new territory for me and I found it very stimulating. It was invigorating to talk about subjects that weren't likely to come up on tour. I missed those nights, but it was time to turn pro.

I'd never seen anything like I saw in Milwaukee at my first tournament as a pro. Back at the L.A. Open that I played when I was sixteen, the first tee was packed, and there was a big fuss around me at the beginning of my round. Then everyone went to watch the top guys once I started playing; I learned to deal with big crowds but was also fine with playing when the spectators moved on. Milwaukee was totally different. The crowds were big all the way through. It was so different from a regular tour event in that most of the spectators were following my group only. It was trippy. In Milwaukee I ripped my first drive 336 yards down the fairway—it was a great feeling.

I played with Bruce Lietzke in one round, and I looked forward to that because he hit everything with a big fade. Even then, you didn't see golfers curving the ball that much. If anything, it was a slight fade or draw. But he hit these big slices out there. I'd heard about the way he played, and had seen it in telecasts. But it was different to experience it. He hit it so far left to a back left pin on one hole that I thought the ball was gone. I was about to yell fore, when all of a sudden the ball started slicing and coming back, and it finished ten feet from the hole. Okay, I thought, I didn't see that coming. This was just another sign that tour players had a lot of game. I mean every tour player. Nobody got to the tour on luck.

It seemed like I played every week after I turned pro, which was much different from playing maybe one or two college tournaments a month. I wanted to win my PGA Tour card for 1997, which meant I needed to keep playing. I tied for sixtieth in Milwaukee, finished eleventh the next week in the rain-shortened Canadian Open, which went three rounds, tied for fifth at the Quad Cities Open, and for third at the B.C. Open in Endicott, New York, my fourth tournament since I became a professional. The tournament was shortened to three rounds because of poor weather. My earnings through the first four tournaments guaranteed that I would finish the year in the top 150 money winners. That meant I could be given unlimited sponsors' exemptions in 1997. All the guys at the B.C. Open were congratulating me on getting my card so fast. That was the coolest thing ever.

Now I was a real tour pro. I'd secured my playing card and gotten my money clip—the recognition in a tangible form that I had made it to the PGA Tour. I won the Las Vegas Invitational two weeks later, finished third at the Texas Open, and then won Disney in October. I was getting tired, because I'd never played as many tournaments in college. Maybe it's crazy to think about a twenty-year-old getting burned out, but that was how I began to feel after Disney. After I got some rest at the end of the year, I won the Mercedes Championships, the tournament reserved for the previous season's winners, at the start of 1997.

I was pointing to the Masters by then, and my education in the short game around Augusta definitely continued on Monday of tournament week. I played nine holes with Seve and Ollie. It was a master class, and when I thought about it, their games reminded me in some ways of the improvisational jazz my dad loved. He appreciated when the talent meshed various musical elements and made something out of nothing. You couldn't practice improvisational jazz, because it would then be something else. You could practice all kinds of shots at Augusta, but inevitably you would put yourself in a spot that you hadn't been in before. Seve and Ollie were geniuses at improvising, and they were Masters champions, with Seve, as I've said, winning in 1980 and 1983, and Ollie in 1994 (he would also win in 1999). They gave me a nine-hole lesson in inventive shot making. I was pumped after playing the nine holes with them. When they continued to play on their own after, I, too, tried all kinds of shots.

A while later I heard a story about Seve that captured his spirit, competitiveness, and creativity. He was playing with Tom Kite in the last round of the '86 Masters, and they were on the par-5 eighth hole. Not many guys could get to the green in two shots then—the ball had yet to turn into an exploding missile. Tom had laid up to about one hundred yards, while Seve's second got him within fifty yards of the green. That right there taught me one thing. It wasn't important to Seve to make sure he had a full shot into a green. If he had to hit half or three-quarter shots, fine. I think he enjoyed those far more than full shots. He always wanted to do something with the golf ball. Conventional, by the exact yardage golf, wasn't for him. Seve was the ultimate feel player. I'd appreciated his style since I first met him, and I wasn't surprised to hear this story—especially when I thought about the shots he hit when we played on the Monday of the '97 Masters.

Kite, I learned, hit a full wedge to the green back on that Sunday in 1986, and holed it. I could just see Seve looking at Tom after he holed his shot, and then thinking about the crafty shot he was about to play. He had something special in mind. I could see his wizardry at play.

Seve then studied his own shot. The hole was cut to the left of a slightly raised portion of the green. Seve had at least a couple of options. He could fly the ball directly at the hole with some sort of shot, and put some spin on the ball to make sure it stopped quickly. But he saw another way. He could use the contours to the right of the hole. Seve chipped the ball up to the green in such a way that it would take the slope and curl toward the hole. I doubt he had practiced that shot, but I'd bet he saw the trajectory and the bounces and the roll clearly in his mind's eye. The ball scooted along the fairway, hit the green running, took the slope, rolled left and sideways, and fell into the hole on top of Tom's ball. They had each holed their approaches and eagled the hole. The way I heard the story, you never saw two happier guys. They walked to the green side by side, acknowledging the people who were watching. It's too bad that CBS wasn't covering that hole. It must have been quite a moment, vintage Seve.

The genius of Augusta National is that it allows you to be so imaginative around the greens. The more creative I could be, the more inspired I would feel. This was another reason I was so excited about my first Masters, and my first major, as a professional golfer.

Chapter Four

Tuesday, April 8, 1997

The interview room in the media center was jammed. It was Tuesday, midafternoon, and my press conference was about to start. I had played an early-morning practice round with Marko, and was glad to get inside the ropes, which had increasingly become a haven for me.

The media's interest in me was already ratcheting up by the time I played the '95 Amateur in Newport, Rhode Island, and then was quite intense by the '96 Amateur at Pumpkin Ridge near Portland. I was going for five USGA events in a row in '95, including two U.S. Amateurs in a row. A few players, including Bobby Jones and Jay Sigel, had won two straight U.S. Amateurs, but I was going for three in a row at Pumpkin Ridge. Interest was so high that about fifteen thousand spectators showed up for my final match against Steve Scott, who played on the University of Florida golf team. I was told that this was the biggest gallery in a U.S. Amateur final since Bobby Jones had gone for the Grand Slam in the 1930 U.S. Amateur at Merion. I was 5 down after the morning eighteen holes in the match against Steve, which, like all U.S. Amateur finals, was scheduled for thirty-six holes, with sudden-death extra holes if necessary. I was still 2 down with three holes to go, but I rallied to be all square after thirty-six, and then I won on the second extra hole.

My main goal, my only goal, all day, was to stay focused. There had been speculation all week about when I planned to turn pro. Would it be right after the tournament? Later? I tried to fend it off by saying I intended to turn pro "in the future." I was still an amateur, and nobody had ever won three straight U.S. Amateurs. It was a completely different deal from going for two in a row, and then it was also going to be for six straight USGA titles. That upped the ante even more. I also happened to shoot 69-67 and qualify for the match-play portion of the tournament as medalist, which meant I was the number one seed.

The interest from fans and media that had been building was at a peak, at least for my amateur career. I needed to get into what my dad called my "major mode," by putting a wall around myself. It felt weird sometimes, as if when I was talking to people, it was somebody else who was talking. I could hear myself talking, while I was thinking about my game at the same time; there was an out-of-body quality about these times. I just didn't want to get out of the cocoon of concentration. I enjoyed being there, and I needed all the focus and mental strength that I could muster. Then I won, and I was exhausted. But what a great feeling. Three straight U.S. Juniors followed by three straight U.S. Amateurs.

I announced two days after the win that I was turning pro. And now, seven and a half months later, I was at Augusta to play the Masters. It didn't surprise me that the media interest had increased so much that the interview room was standing room only. This was flattering, but at the same time, I had been on a mission for years not to let the interest go to my head.

The press conference got off to an odd start, in that my response to the first question made for an uneasy moment in the room. Danny Yates, an Augusta member, was running the room during my interview, and said, "Well, we've got what y'all have been waiting for all day. So, Tiger, say a few words, and we'll let them have a go at you."

I answered exactly as he asked, with three words: "Hi and bye." I was messing around, but then again, that's how my dad taught me to answer questions from the media. If they asked me what club I hit into a green, I gave the number of the club. I wouldn't elaborate and say something like, "I hit seven-iron. I was thinking eight, but I felt some wind come up and I didn't want to take a chance of it knocking the ball down and leaving it in the front bunker." Nope, I was asked what club I hit, and I answered. That was it. I realized this wasn't the way to become popular with the media, but that's the approach my dad had taught me to employ. But I also wanted to be respectful at the Masters when asked a question. I knew Mr. Yates was asking for more than "Hi and bye."

My answer still wasn't full of information. That wasn't my nature, and never would be. I said, "No, I guess as always, it's a pleasure to be here at Augusta. I'm definitely looking forward to playing." I could see the collective yawn in front of me. I wasn't known as a "good quote" or a "good interview." At that point Mr. Yates opened the floor up to questions. Right away I was asked about whether tour life was as demanding as I thought it would be. I went into default mode and answered, "No, a lot more." It took a follow-up question of "Travel, media, autographs, what?" to draw me out. I wasn't trying to be cagey or play with the media, but I was wary. I was looking out at a sea of reporters, and didn't know many of them. I didn't know who I could trust, and so I wasn't going to say whatever came into my mind.

I preferred to be insulated from the world outside the ropes, though I knew I couldn't live like that. Maybe I would ease up with the media. It was still so early in my pro career that I wasn't sure how it would go. I didn't want to let anybody outside my circle of close friends and family—anybody—inside my head. But I recognized that I had media obligations. I was trying to find a balance between the private and the public. I hadn't found it, and I'm not sure I ever have.

In looking at the transcript of that Tuesday interview, I see that I felt the same way then as I had for years, as an amateur. The travel, media, and autographs were why tour life was more demanding than life as an amateur. I said something I had always believed and felt, that "the golf part is actually the easiest part. That part, I love to do." I went on to say that it was difficult to satisfy everybody who wanted a piece of my time, and that I had learned to say no.

In a way, it was a feat that I could even speak at these big media gatherings, or in public at all, because I had stuttered badly as a kid in elementary school. My stuttering was so noticeable, and it made me feel so anxious, that I made sure to sit at the back of the classroom hoping that my teachers wouldn't call on me. Why would you sit in the front row if you couldn't speak? My mind worked, but I couldn't get the words out from my mind to my mouth. Anytime I had to speak, I stuttered so badly that I gave up.

Eventually, Mom took me to a speech therapist. The speech therapist concluded that hearing two languages (English and Thai) at a young age confused me, and led to the stuttering. I went to a special after-school program for two years to learn how to speak comfortably. All through school, I continued to fight through my stuttering problem so I could develop the confidence to apply to a top university. I even talked to my dog, a half Lab and half retriever named Boom-Boom—he was named that because his voice was so loud for a little pup. He listened to me until he fell asleep. Learning how to stop stuttering was a lot tougher than changing my swing, that's for sure.

Many years later, in 2015, I learned about a youngster who stuttered, from an article in *Golf Digest* by Ron Sirak. The boy stuttered so badly that he tried to commit suicide because he was bullied; his parents stopped him just before he jumped from his bedroom window, but he fractured his ankle while being pulled back. I found out that he liked to watch me on television. So I got his name and wrote a letter encouraging him, and reassuring him that he too could overcome his stuttering. The former LPGA Tour player Sophie Gustafson—who also stutters—was mentoring the boy, and Ron had written about this. What a wonderful and generous thing for Sophie to do.

As for me, looking back, I can only say that to go from sitting at the back of a classroom because of fear, to going to Stanford, to sitting in front of two hundred people in the media center and answering questions, even reluctantly, well, I thought I had come a long way.

The press conference lasted quite a while. I enjoyed the bits where we talked about the course and strategy, and pointed out that I thought Masters winners had one thing in common: They kept the ball below the hole. It was impossible to score at Augusta if you were putting from above the hole. I had that lesson burned into me for all time when I putted off the first green that first round of my first Masters two years before. The trick to playing Augusta was to never hit your approach to where the ball would stay above the hole. That meant, as I said, that you had to be very strategic in your iron play. "That's set up for your tee shots, too," I said. "You can't just fire it down the fairway and hope for the best. You have to place your tee shots." Mo was showing me that in our morning practice round. You could never learn that enough. I kept these ideas at the forefront of my mind as I moved toward the first round.

* * *

Augusta makes it easy to focus on your preparation. The Masters does the best job of any tournament in the world of helping shield players from the spotlight. The practice grounds were clear of people except for instructors and caddies, and in general they did a tremendous job of protecting the players. Television crews weren't allowed on the range, and the same went for other media. You could get your practice done without distraction, which was not the case at other tournaments. Pro golfers are lucky to have the fame and the media glare that come with it, and I have never forgotten that. But at the same time, the practice areas and the putting green were our offices, where we did the work that made us worth watching in the first place. I'm not the only player who would like more privacy on the practice ranges at PGA Tour events.

On the course, at Augusta, it was only the player

and his caddie, nobody else. The media were allowed inside the ropes at PGA Tour events, but not at the Masters, not even during practice rounds. Even the instructors weren't allowed inside the ropes. Butchie walked with the gallery, outside the ropes. If I wanted to talk to him, I walked over to him.

My practice round in the morning with Marko had gone well. Augusta was all about where you placed your drives, based on where the pins were that day. If the hole was cut on the front of the green at nine, I wanted to be sure to hit my approach past the hole and not put so much spin on the ball that it would roll back the steep slope and off the green—something that happened to Norman in the last round of the '96 Masters. Thinking about another hole, the seventeenth, I didn't want to short-side myself if the pin was on the right side of the green. That was an almost impossible up and down. Still, I could see where it would be difficult to go through an entire Masters without making some mistakes, especially into the greens. I tried to learn where to miss the ball so that I could have a decent chance of getting up and down. The guys I'd played practice rounds with knew what to do at Augusta with their short games, so I asked mostly short-game questions. The easy part was blowing my drives over the top of the fairway bunkers. The hard part was to decide where to miss my approaches to each flag, and if I did miss it, what shot to play from there. There were no excuses for me to miss all of these types of shots in those ways. Especially not after playing in the Masters before, and not after having practice rounds with many of the best players in the game, including former winners.

One of the elements that I was able to use to my advantage was the ball I used at that time, which was the Titleist Professional 90. It had a liquid core and wound construction, with a cast urethane cover. The ball spun a lot, and I could do quite a bit with it. However, I could also get into trouble with it when I made a bad swing, because the ball moved much more in the wind. It would drift on the wind, even if I hit a shot where I was trying to hold it up against the wind. But around the greens, it was the perfect ball for Augusta. It also helped that we were using square grooves then, which allowed for more spin.

While I had signed with Titleist when I turned pro, the arrangement was that I could play any clubs I wanted until Titleist developed equipment for me. (I was already using a Titleist ball.) I used Mizuno MP29s in my two-, three-, and four-irons, and MP14s from the five-iron through the pitching wedge. My sand wedge and sixty-degree were Cleveland Classic. I also played with a King Cobra

10.5-degree driver, and a Titleist PT, fifteen-degree three-wood. My putter was a Scotty Cameron with the teryllium insert. It resembled the PING Anser 2 that I had used for years. Every putter I have used looks like the Anser 2, because I grew up with that putter. I liked the slight offset that allowed me to have my hands just ahead of the ball at impact. And the plumber's neck made sense for me, because my stroke moved on an arc.

I felt totally comfortable with my equipment, maybe because I didn't mess around much with it. All that mattered to me was that the clubs delivered when I made the swings I wanted. Augusta would expose any weaknesses if I didn't have more than a few different shots in my repertoire. I had the three wedges in my bag, and this gave me enough options for shots depending on the lie around the greens. My pitching wedge was fifty-one degrees, and I also carried a fifty-six sand wedge and a sixty. The fifty-six and sixty were the only clubs in my bag that had square grooves. I liked the V grooves in the rest of my irons, especially on courses where there was rough. I was fine with fliers out of the rough, and I had learned how to control a flier.

Around the greens, though, it was a different story. I wanted to know exactly how far I could pitch the ball with various lengths of swing at differing speeds. I wanted to know how the ball would react when it hit the green. After my practice round Tuesday, I couldn't see myself using the sixty except out of greenside bunkers when I did short-side myself. I hoped that wouldn't happen. It all depended on where I placed my drives. If I gave myself the proper angles to the pins, I could avoid being in many bunkers.

* * *

I had learned during my practice rounds that I could play different angles at Augusta. It wasn't only a matter of standing up and bombing it down the middle of the fairway, because there was so much room before the club added rough—the "second cut"—and before it lengthened the course for the 2002 Masters. Trees were also added, and as the course changed, so did the way I viewed it. It was becoming less of an inland links and more of a parkland course. But it was still an inland links back in '97, which meant I could pick and choose from a wide variety of shots.

The eleventh hole often comes to mind when I think back on the way the course was playing. I could drive the ball far to the right, both because the fairway was so wide and there weren't any trees to speak of on that side. From there I had an ideal angle into the green, and I didn't even have to think about the water on the left. It didn't come into play from the right side, even from where the gallery was.

Ben Hogan used to say that if he hit the green with his second shot, you knew he had made a mistake because he never went for the green. Hogan was hitting a mid or long iron for his second shot, and so he was only being smart when he played right of the green and away from the pond to the left. I was hitting the ball so far that I was using a short iron or wedge into the green. Playing from the right side and with that short a club in my hands allowed me to hit my approach to the green, and sometimes directly to the hole. If I missed the green, you knew I'd made a mistake. If the flag was on the right-hand side of the green, I drove to the middle left of the fairway, and then played to the middle left of the green. The strategy worked for me. I was playing a different course than Hogan had played, not because Augusta National had changed the course—yet—but because I was hitting the ball so far and because the course was so spacious.

* * *

Even in my amateur days, I was never much of a guy for hanging around the course after I played a tournament round, or, for that matter, a practice round. The only reason I ever stayed was to practice. Otherwise, I was out of there. I saw no reason to change after I turned pro. I did what I had to do in terms of any media obligations, such as the press conference, or any interviews with the various networks that had the television rights to the Masters. Jerry drove me home after the press conference Tuesday. I wasn't one to nap, so that was out. We played some hoops, a lot of Ping-Pong, and some video games. I needed those distractions. I didn't want to be thinking about the Masters every minute during the week. The week of the Masters itself was a time for me to practice, sure, but I was there to play the tournament, not to find my game.

The house was chill. It was that way all week, because I was home with my friends and family. We got to hang out and have a good time. If I had stayed in college, I'd have been a junior. Instead, I was a tour pro at the Masters. My pretournament media conference was over, and I felt it had gone well. The atmosphere had loosened up after the way it started. Now it was my job to play well enough for a return visit, or a few return visits, to the media center.

Chapter Five

Wednesday, April 9, 1997

When I woke up Wednesday morning, I felt the excitement I'd become used to when an important tournament was approaching. Golf's a weird game. You need to feel both a sense of power when you want to rip a drive down there, and almost subdued when you're facing a delicate shot over a bunker to a pin just on the other side, with the green running away from you. I had learned to control my heart rate through breathing, not that this was ever easy.

I wanted explosiveness to drive the ball at Augusta, so that I'd come in with the wedges that would give me an advantage. I studied what goes into being explosive, something that would continue as I got older. It was a matter of developing fast-twitch muscle fibers, which I worked on by doing power lifting in the gym. The most effective way of doing this is by lifting heavy weights at a fast pace. Although you're born with fast twitch, you can also develop it. Sprinting also helps develop fast-twitch muscles, so I did that as well. In both cases, the key is to have a training program that mixes short duration with high intensity. Developing fast-twitch muscles helped me really tear through the ball from the top of my backswing.

What also takes a lot of work is going from fast twitch to slow twitch in the space of a few minutes, from bombing a drive to that tricky little pitch shot to Augusta's slick, undulating greens. It's much easier to develop slow twitch than fast twitch. I trained to develop more slow-twitch muscle fibers by doing long endurance runs, and by lifting at a slower rate of speed than when training fast twitch. I also did more reps. I always looked forward to spending time in the gym, often for hours.

I was only twenty-one, but I knew my nature. I was high-strung. I wanted to feel the adrenaline while playing tournament golf, but also to be able to calm myself down at will. Marko and I would talk a lot about this from the time we first met. He'd won all over the world, but he hadn't won any majors. It was hard to win majors—or any tournaments, for that matter—but I wondered whether he thought any factors in particular had kept him from winning those. I was curious why a player of his caliber hadn't won a major. He didn't know, but it certainly wasn't for lack of trying.

One of the mysteries of tournament golf, or of any sport, is why some players have a knack for winning, and winning a lot. There's an intangible factor, and it's difficult to come to grips with what it is.

Marko didn't mind my asking why he hadn't won a major, though. He was like a big brother to me, a mentor in many ways. We had the sort of friendship in which we could talk about anything. Still, it was apparent he didn't want to be hung with that "best player not to win a major" tag. But we could also joke around and give it to one another.

Although the crowds were massive during every practice round, they seemed even bigger to me on Wednesday. Maybe it was the magnitude of the occasion, but I felt all eyes were on me. That made me uneasy, although you would think I would have adjusted to it by that time; still I felt uncomfortable. Mo helped me deal with the attention. He showed me that I could get in the practice I wanted, hit my shots, but still be relaxed and even kid around with the people watching. I tried to do that, but I was also locking in more and more so that I could get to the first tee Thursday in the frame of mind I wanted. I was hitting the ball the way I wanted during my last practice round. I was getting into that state where, when I'm playing, I'm in my tournament armor. But in practice I did want to be able to enjoy the moment, and to enjoy the people watching me. I wasn't always successful, especially after I hit a shot I didn't like. But I did try. If I was going to succeed in majors, I had better get used to the attention.

Marko saw what was going on. On the ninth tee, he said to me, "Can you imagine if you had five bucks for every picture people are taking of you?" We kept playing, and I was very careful to watch him on the greens. He was a very good putter, so I observed how he played the right amount of break and speed. He was a control player, and so I also watched to see where and when he decided to be aggressive based on where the holes were cut.

My friend Jay Brunza had also helped me prepare for the Masters. He helped me control my creativity. I sometimes wanted to do too much with a shot, instead of hitting a conventional shot. Augusta could trick you into wanting to play a funky shot even if the circumstances didn't require it. Why mess around when you have a stock shot in front of you? Then again, how do you maintain the balance between playing creative golf and what might be called standard golf?

Jay also helped me understand that I wasn't good at visualizing a shot. Sports psychologists and mental coaches have advised for years that you should see the shot before you play it. But I couldn't do that. I never could, and I still can't. I couldn't say to myself, "Okay, this is the trajectory I see, this is how the shape of the shot will look." My mind would run away. I saw too much, which isn't helpful in golf. I instead had to learn, and to accept, that my nature was to feel a shot with my hands and my body. I felt what I wanted my hands to do at impact, and trusted that the feeling would create the motion to hit the ball to the spot I wanted. In contrast, Jack Nicklaus didn't pull the club back until he saw the shot he wanted or, on the green, until he saw the ball going into the hole. I didn't understand how he did that, just as I'm sure he didn't understand my approach.

* * *

As the first round approached, I was concerned about one aspect of my swing. I was very flashy through the ball because I was so far across the line at the top of my backswing. I had worked hard with Butchie on my swing plane, and it had improved dramatically. But I still found myself having problems getting on plane. I had to save my impact position with my hands, which is what I mean by being "flashy." My arms and body weren't feeling in sync, which was crucial to go hard at the ball or ease up for a soft shot. Butchie and I had worked on the problem the week before Augusta, and I'd also tried to watch Marko closely. Maybe his control would rub off on me, I thought.

In the meantime, I relied on timing my impact position with my hands. To get the face in the position to hit the shot I wanted, I dumped my hands a little under the plane coming through. It looked like I was dropping my hands in front of me. I reminded myself, though, that I had shot 59 the week before, and that I had come in swinging well. I wasn't far off coming into the week. I had things dialed in nicely. But golf being golf, I had slipped a little.

I didn't tell anybody but Butchie that I was afraid of hooking the ball as the first round approached. I was fighting a hook up to Augusta, getting stuck and flippy. I got to a point where I was striping my driver in practice, but would it hold up under the gun? Would it really work? I had enough doubt in my mind that I wondered when a bad drive would come out and head left. I was getting stuck, and there didn't seem to be much I could do about it except hope that my timing was on during the tournament.

It wasn't as if I hadn't worked consistently on improving my plane. It was a work in progress, and I figured maybe it always would be. I had started the game so early that it wasn't easy to find equipment that worked well. Individualized club fitting wasn't nearly as popular, or as sophisticated, when I was a five-year-old in 1980. My dad organized my clubs, and he did the best he could with what was known in my early days. He took a person he considered average in size, somewhere around six feet tall, and did a proportionality slide of how long a club should be based on a person's height. Pop came up with what he was looking for. Because of that I had clubs that fit me, so I didn't have to make the bad swing adjustments that kids made to clubs that didn't fit them.

But there was one problem with the clubs: They were heavy. My dad cut down his clubs, in which the shafts were X-100 as they were measured. They were cut down to a size where I could use them, but they were still heavy. Thus, when I first started, I had to learn how to create all the power and speed out of my body when using this heavy equipment. I was too small and weak as a kid to do this with my hands alone, so I used my hips to create the speed.

As I progressed, the shaft never flexed for me, or if it did flex, I didn't feel it. It just came about. I didn't

107

force it. And as I got older, this technique helped me move my hips faster in my downswing and through impact. These methods, plus what I can only describe as instinct, must have led me to figure out a way to get the club back to the ball in as square a position as possible, and to do so with speed.

When my dad switched me over to clubs that were close to regular length when I was thirteen, I freaked out. I felt the shaft kick for the first time. I couldn't time the shaft to get back to the ball properly. Suddenly, the shaft was flexing when I took it back. I wondered what was going on, and asked my dad. He told me it was the flex in the shaft working, and that I would hit the ball a lot farther once I started timing it right. I didn't know if I needed to speed up or slow down. Eventually I figured it out, but it took a long time. Coming into the Masters, I still tended to spin my hips so fast sometimes that I would outrun my hands. That was why my plane went wonky.

When I was playing well, I could feel exactly what my body was doing during my swing and what was wrong when I was out of position. The science says it's impossible to make a change inside of a motion that takes a second and a half or so. But I believed I could make the compensation. On the way down, or halfway down, or right before impact, I could fix what was wrong. I could save the shot with my hands. As it turned out, that came in handy during the Masters.

My dad had taught me how to save a shot by ordering me at the top of my swing to hit a particular type of shot: a draw, or a big hook, or a fade, or a big slice. That was just fun and games, but it trained me to be able to save the shot when things weren't going well. "Oh man, I made a terrible backswing there. What could I do? I'm going to have to slide my hips a bit forward to delay the hit, or else this ball is going dead left." Or other times, "Dammit, I really have to release my hips and open them up. I have to push off my right foot. Okay, I have to delay my hands, slow down my upper body, or I need to speed up my left arm, or my right arm, extend it now." I felt all those things as I learned to save the shot. To me, that's being in the moment.

Now, this doesn't mean I could compete at the highest levels with that action all the time. But it was encouraging to know I had it in me, especially when I wasn't in sync during my practice rounds and practice sessions. Butchie put me through a full-swing drill that I didn't like from the moment we started working together. The drill was meant to help me improve my plane by getting my arms and body working together. He felt I needed to learn to keep my arms more in front of me throughout my swing. That way I would be less reliant on timing. It would also improve my plane because my arms and hands weren't flipping the club off plane.

Butchie had me take the club to the top and stop there. The next step was to rock back with some momentum, then start down and complete my swing. I was not fond of this drill, because it was impossible to create any speed when I stopped my swing. I was young. I liked power, and I had it—even if it was created through flash instead of a smooth transfer of energy.

But the drill wasn't about power. I lost all momentum when I stopped the club at the top. Rocking back produced very little momentum. I wasn't making a golf swing. I was stopping and starting to find a position that would promote consistency. The point was for me to feel where the club was at the top, and then to let it go from there in conjunction with my body. The drill was about developing a feel, and the proper sequence from the position at the top as a means of creating accuracy and speed. The drill did improve my sequence, and more important, I got the feel of where I wanted the club at the top. It was often rough going, and frustrating, but I eventually got to where I could do it naturally, without thinking about it.

I still tended to fall back into the habits I'd learned when I started golf with clubs that were too heavy for me. That wasn't going away, not for good, anyway. Every golfer has faults he will have to monitor for his entire career. My major error of getting stuck started when I was a kid, and it wasn't going to disappear entirely. Ever.

* * *

The Par 3 Contest was on Wednesday afternoon, as it had been for years. It's one of those traditions that make the Masters unique. The Par 3 course is beautiful. I played the Par 3 every year through 2004, when I got a hole in one on the ninth hole while playing with Mo and Arnold. I shot 23 that year and tied for the low score with Pádraig Harrington. Nobody had won the Par 3 and gone on to win the Masters in the same year. I wasn't going to test the historical record, and I bowed to superstition. I chose not to play off for the crystal that the club gives to the winner. In addition to the superstition, I felt the Par 3 was a distraction from the tournament, and maybe a bit too close to the first round for me. I stopped playing after 2004, but after my children Sam and Charlie were born, I decided I'd play again when they were old enough to caddie for me. Sam was seven and Charlie was six in 2015, when I played the Par 3 again. I was glad I did.

Over the years, the Par 3 Contest had become quite a family event, with kids, grandkids, wives, and other family members caddying. It was more of a gambling event when I first played it. Guys would play with their buddies, and usually for a pretty good amount. Some serious amounts of cash were exchanged in the locker rooms. That still happens, but not nearly as much, not with the kids around.

I played the Par 3 in 1997 with Tom Kite, and, luckily, I didn't win. It was such a pretty nine holes, playing around two ponds. Many of the banks around the tiny greens were shaved like on the main course. If you missed a green, the ball rolled away into the water.

The Par 3 course at Augusta hasn't changed since I first played it. The holes are the same lengths, seventy to 135 yards. Maybe there's a lesson here; there's more to the game than length. Sure, the Par 3 Course is meant for fun and it's not supposed to be a tournament course. But when I think of some of the best holes in golf, many are short par-3s: The seventh at Pebble Beach is barely over one hundred yards and is one of the most entertaining and challenging holes in golf. Tour pros don't like to have to hit half shots. But that's what we hit on most of the holes at the Par 3 course.

Then there's the par-3, 155-yard twelfth at Augusta. It's one of the few holes that hasn't changed at Augusta National since I played the '97 Masters. If I wanted a chance to win the Masters, I would have to get past the hole without making a mistake. Rae's Creek in front; the bank in front that feeds balls hit just a bit short into the water; the bunkers in front and behind, with the green running from back to front.

Many factors make the twelfth one of the outstanding holes in the game. It's in a perfect spot in a corner of the course, for one thing. The wind can come down the eleventh hole, which goes in the same direction, and also from the thirteenth, moving in the opposite direction. The winds seem to converge on the twelfth. The twelfth green, meanwhile, is offset just enough to complicate the tee shot that much more. I used to hear that the time to hit your tee shot was when the flags on the eleventh and twelfth were synched up, but I found that wasn't true, because the wind on twelve can still play havoc with your ball. You just have to be committed to your shot, and then hope for the best.

Another influence on the shot is that the carry

distance to the green changes from the front left to the back right of the green. If the green weren't offset, the twelfth would still be a visually stunning hole because of Rae's Creek in front, the backdrop of trees and flowers, and the dazzling white sand in the front and rear bunkers. But the hole itself would be bland without the green being offset.

* * *

Finally, the day of the first round arrived. My starting time for the first round was 1:44, with Nick Faldo. Steve Stricker and Paul Stankowski were in the twosome ahead, and Ollie and Marko were in the twosome behind. Okay, let's go.

Chapter Six

Thursday, April 10, 1997

I would never have believed that I would shoot 40 on the front nine of the first round, but I did. My practice had gone well enough; my dad had given me that putting advice Wednesday night, and I warmed up nicely before I started. My routine was as per usual. I went for my morning run. I got to the practice green an hour and twenty minutes before my 1:44 starting time and putted for about twenty minutes. I worked on the two-tee drill that I had used since I was eight years old. I placed one tee at the heel and one tee at the toe of the head of the putter, with the ball slightly ahead. The putter fit, just barely, between the tees. The practice was to help me make the putter go through without hitting the tees. I was looking for a pure hit, right in the center of the head. I didn't care about the path of the putter. I cared only about where I hit the ball, and not contacting the tees. I also stroked some putts with my right hand alone, because I wanted to promote the slight release of the head. I wasn't a dead-hand putter. There was always that slight release, a hardly noticeable hit. It was there when I putted well, and I felt it.

After putting, I went to the short-game area that was then on the other side of the range, next to the Par 3 course. I chipped for a few minutes, and hit some sand shots before I went to the range. I went through my bag as Butchie and Fluff watched, and came back to the short-game area to hit a few more chip shots. We didn't talk much as I warmed up, and when we did, it was the usual stuff: sports, a few jokes. My objective was to get a feel for the shots. I hit a few more balls, with the last one being a rehearsal with my driver for the first shot I would soon hit in the tournament. Then I walked to the putting green behind the first tee, and I hit some putts for about five minutes before getting to the first tee a few minutes before my starting time.

I was totally absorbed in the first shot. It was as if nobody else was there, and yet the spectators had to be ten deep around the tee and back to the clubhouse. All I saw was the first fairway stretching away from the tee. I was focused on where I needed to place the golf ball and how I would place it to set up the next shot from the proper angle, to either attack the pin or play a defensive shot. I had drifted into my own little world.

So what did I do? I hit a high drive way left and into the trees—the shot I feared. Maybe I shouldn't have been surprised. Butchie and I had observed that even though I'd rehearsed it, I often hit a poor shot right out of the gate. Sometimes I was just too amped up at the start of a round, and it felt as though I had to get the first shot out of my system before I could settle down and get into the rhythm of the round.

I had no shot to the green from the trees, but managed to play my second into the bunker left of the green. I couldn't get it up and down from the bunker, and so I started the Masters with a bogey. That was a bit unsettling but nothing to worry about. Things didn't get better, though. They were unraveling, and I was getting annoyed, even hot, at myself. What was going on? I bogeyed the fourth when I missed the green so far to the right it was almost in the bamboo trees over there. I don't think people even knew there was bamboo over there, fifty yards off line. A palm tree was also there, supposedly the only one on the property. I banged my ball out of there, bogeyed the hole, and was 2 over, just like that. Then, on the par-5 eighth, I really started to come apart. I hit my tee shot way left into the trees again. Somehow I planted my feet in an awkward stance around the ball, which was resting on pine straw. My six-iron got back to the fairway, and from there I hit a four-iron over the green and made my third bogey. My tee shot on the ninth was a snap hook into the trees, which led to another bogey. I thought to myself, "That's how you shoot 40 on the front nine at Augusta."

I was surrounded by a half-dozen or so Pinkerton security guards as I walked off the ninth green and over to the tenth tee. I could now feel everybody's eyes on me. I was dimly aware that some were saying the tournament was already over for me. My dad's military experience helped me here. He taught me to be completely aware of my surroundings, while maintaining complete focus on the task at hand. On the ninth green, I was totally aware of my surroundings, but I chose to not acknowledge anybody there as I walked to the tenth tee. What would be the point?

Fluff reminded me we had played only nine holes. There was plenty of time to turn things around, but we still had a long way to go. Although he reassured me of his belief that I could do it, I was far inside my own head, trying to understand what had gone wrong. I realized my backswing had gotten too long, but I didn't want to force my swing into a position. Instead, I focused on what I wanted my swing to feel like on the back nine. It should feel as it did when I shot that 59 with Marko the week before at Isleworth, I thought. It wasn't as if I hadn't had to call on mental resources before. I tried to draw on my memories of being behind in the final matches of the U.S. Junior and U.S. Amateur championships that I had won, and to call on the feelings I had while busting through the 60 mark at Isleworth. I needed to draw on the mental strength I'd developed, under the guidance of my parents, and translate it into a better swing.

* * *

The mental training for golf that my dad had put me through proved itself during that short walk from the ninth green to the tenth tee, and was completely vindicated by the way I played on the back nine. He had trained me to be what he sometimes called a "cold-blooded assassin" on the course, by applying more of the principles he had learned and used while in the military. I needed this training if I was going to be able to deal with life as a professional golfer, with life as the supposed "black hope" in the game, with life as somebody who had won championships as an amateur, and of whom big things were expected. I expected them of myself—in fact, there was no way the expectations of others exceeded my own. Maybe it sounded arrogant when I said I entered every tournament to win, and that I expected to win. But that was how I felt, and I wasn't going to pretend otherwise.

From early on, I wanted to make myself as tough-minded as possible. When I was about eleven, I asked my dad to help me get there. As I was always so small and scrawny, I felt I needed the upper hand in other ways. The only way I could beat others as a junior, even inside my age group, where I might be up against kids a few years older, was to never make a mental mistake, and to out-tough them. So, I told my dad, "Okay, toughen me up." That was when he started what he called "psychological warfare" and "prisoner of war" techniques with me.

Pop would push me to the point where I might not feel as confident in myself. He tried to make me feel insecure. Later, I would learn that others thought he was doing this without my permission, but that's not true. I needed him to push me to the edge of not wanting to continue because I had to

A balanced swing with the driver. Freedom and balance make for an effective combination, which usually produces length and accuracy. (Sam Greenwood/ Getty Images)

Mark O'Meara, my friend, mentor, and in 1998, a Masters champion. This must have been a good shot. (Sam Greenwood/Getty Images)

Short game master José María Olazábal showed me an array of shots when we practiced together. (Sam Greenwood/Getty Images)

On the putting green with two-time Masters winner Ben Crenshaw. Has anybody looked more comfortable with a putter in his hands? (Timothy A. Clary /Getty Images)

I've just driven from the fifteenth tee in the first round. The shot worked out: I eagled the par-five after my long drive. (Phil Sheldon/Popperfoto/Getty Images)

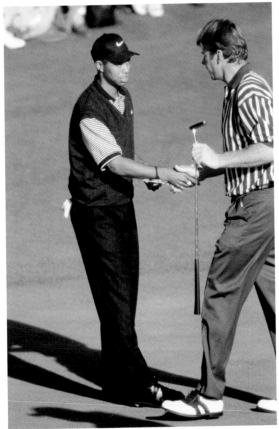

Nick Faldo, the 1989, 1990, and 1996 Masters winner, was one of the game's best "control" players. He was an intense competitor, and we didn't talk much during the first round. (Augusta National Historic Imagery)

In the middle of it all, with Paul Azinger, putting in the second round. I'm lost in thought. (Augusta National Historic Imagery)

Colin Montgomerie is full of personality, and he shows it. (Augusta National Historic Imagery)

I often studied putts this way, the better to frame the line and keep everything else outside. (Augusta National Historic Imagery)

REPLACE DIVOTS / SMOOTH TRAPS — SCORER

FIX BALL MARKS ON GREENS — ATTESTED

DATE 5-29-8_

	YARDS											YARDS											RATING 50.1
YARDS	128	135	91	126	125	121	121	140	150	1140		119	103	85	130	85	118	119	136	121	1016	2156	RATING 50.1
PAR	3	3	3	3	3	3	3	3	3	27		3	3	3	3	3	3	3	3	3	27	54	
STROKE HOLE	5	3	17	7	13	15	11	9	1			10	18	14	2	16	12	6	4	8			
Tiger Woods	2	4	3	4	3	3	4	3	3	29		3	3	1	4	4	3	3	5	3	29	58	(6 YRS
Brian Merkna	3	3	3	3	4	3	3	3	3	27		3	3	5	4	3	4	4	3	3	32	59	(14 YRS
Joe Marando	4	4	4	4	4	5	4	3	4	36		3	3	4	3	4	5	3	3	4	31	67	15 YRS
HOLE	1	2	3	4	5	6	7	8	9	OUT		10	11	12	13	14	15	16	17	18	IN	TOT	HDC	NET
Demetri George	5	3	2	3	3	3	3	3	4	29		4	3	4	3	4	3	3	4		31	60	15 YRS
Robert Stolar	5	3	4	3	3	3	3	4	4	31		3	4	3	4	3	2	3	3	3	28	59	15 YRS

U.S.G.A.RULES GOVERN ALL PLAY EXCEPT FOR THE FOLLOWING AND POSTED LOCAL RULES.
1. After six strokes, pick up ball, then go to next hole. 2. Players must at all times keep up with the group ahead. 3. Each player must have three clubs including a putter. 4. Play no more than one ball to any green. 5. All water hazards to be played as one stroke penalty. 6. Ball resting on wrong green must not be played on that green, but 20 feet off apron. 7. Ball may be dropped two club lengths away from all protective fences, staked trees or unnatural hazards. No penalty. 8. Players may lay away from fences enclosing course, and driving range, two club lengths-one stroke penalty. 9. High Heels are not permitted on the course. THANK YOU-HAVE A GOOD TIME.

PROFESSIONAL GOLF INSTRUCTION
Ben King - PGA Professional
George Thomsen - Golf Shop Mgr.

LESSONS BY APPOINTMENT
Assistant Professionals
Max Bublitz   John Pard
Shop Assistants
Sandy Carpenter   Tracy Wilkinson

IN THE GOLF SHOP AT HEARTWELL YOU'LL FIND
Name Brand Golf Clubs   New and Used Men's and Ladies'
Free Professional Club Fitting   Starter Sets Available
Gifts available for all occassions--Courtesy wrap   Gift Certificates

My first hole in one, when I was six. Maybe this is why I want short courses to accompany the courses I design. (Courtesy of Mrs. Tida Woods)

Early days on the range with the media. (Courtesy of Mrs. Tida Woods)

The first time I met Sam Snead. (Courtesy of Mrs. Tida Woods)

Even a kid needs to take a break during a round. (Courtesy of Mrs. Tida Woods)

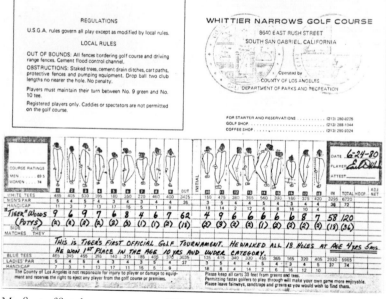

My first official tournament at Whittier Narrows Golf Course. I started with a nine and finished with a seven. Everybody has to start somewhere. (Courtesy of Mrs. Tida Woods)

For as long as I can remember, Mom and Pop were there to support me. (Courtesy of Mrs. Tida Woods)

Notah Begay and me in 1995, during my first visit to Augusta National. We had just arrived after a collegiate tournament. (Courtesy of Mrs. Tida Woods)

My lifelong pal Mikey Gout, Kathy Battaglia, and Pop at the house where I stayed. (Courtesy of Mike Gout)

I enjoyed playing with Costantino Rocca in the final round, and I especially liked his smooth action through the ball. (Sam Greenwood/ Getty Images)

A faraway look. (David Cannon/ Getty Images)

The "patrons" at the Masters know the game and they follow the tournament closely. I felt their encouragement all week. (Timothy A. Clary /Getty Images)

This was the walk up the last fairway I had looked forward to when I imagined winning the Masters. And now I was about to win. I appreciated the standing ovation I got as I neared the green. (Augusta National Historic Imagery)

There it is: My final putt is down. (Augusta National Historic Imagery)

The instant I won. After a week of hard work and the preparation leading up to it, I was ecstatic. (Timothy A. Clary/ Getty Images)

Fluff helped me from the first hole to the last. We share a moment on the last green after I'd putted out. (Augusta National Historic Imagery)

Thanks, Pop. A moment I cherish, a moment I will never forget. (Bob Pearson/Getty Images)

My dad was so ill he wasn't supposed to be at the Masters. But he wasn't going to miss it. The emotions poured out as Mom looked on. (Heinz Kluetmeier/ Getty Images)

MASTERS® TOURNAMENT 1997 OFFICIAL SCORECARD

Tiger Woods — Thursday, April 10, 1997

Hole	1	2	3	4	5	6	7	8	9	Out	10	11	12	13	14	15	16	17	18	In	Totals
Yardage	400	555	360	205	435	180	360	535	435	3465	485	455	155	485	405	500	170	400	405	3460	6925
Par	4	5	4	3	4	3	4	5	4	36	4	4	3	5	4	5	3	4	4	36	72
	5	5	4	4	4	3	4	6	5	40	3	4	2	4	4	3	3	3	4	30	70

Marker's Signature

I HAVE CHECKED MY SCORE HOLE BY HOLE.

Competitor's Signature — Tiger Woods

MASTERS® TOURNAMENT 1997 OFFICIAL SCORECARD

Tiger Woods — Friday, April 11, 1997

Hole	1	2	3	4	5	6	7	8	9	Out	10	11	12	13	14	15	16	17	18	In	Totals
Yardage	400	555	360	205	435	180	360	535	435	3465	485	455	155	485	405	500	170	400	405	3460	6925
Par	4	5	4	3	4	3	4	5	4	36	4	4	3	5	4	5	3	4	4	36	72
	4	4	5	3	3	3	4	4	4	34	4	4	2	3	3	4	3	4	4	32	66

Marker's Signature

I HAVE CHECKED MY SCORE HOLE BY HOLE.

Competitor's Signature — Tiger Woods

MASTERS® TOURNAMENT 1997 OFFICIAL SCORECARD

Tiger Woods — Saturday, April 12, 1997

Hole	1	2	3	4	5	6	7	8	9	Out	10	11	12	13	14	15	16	17	18	In	Totals
Yardage	400	555	360	205	435	180	360	535	435	3465	485	455	155	485	405	500	170	400	405	3460	6925
Par	4	5	4	3	4	3	4	5	4	36	4	4	3	5	4	5	3	4	4	36	72
	4	4	4	3	3	3	3	4	4	32	4	3	3	5	4	4	3	4	3	33	65

Marker's Signature

I HAVE CHECKED MY SCORE HOLE BY HOLE.

Competitor's Signature — Tiger Woods

MASTERS® TOURNAMENT 1997 OFFICIAL SCORECARD

Tiger Woods — Sunday, April 13, 1997

Hole	1	2	3	4	5	6	7	8	9	Out	10	11	12	13	14	15	16	17	18	In	Totals
Yardage	400	555	360	205	435	180	360	535	435	3465	485	455	155	485	405	500	170	400	405	3460	6925
Par	4	5	4	3	4	3	4	5	4	36	4	4	3	5	4	5	3	4	4	36	72
	4	4	4	3	5	3	5	4	4	36	4	3	3	4	3	5	3	4	4	33	69

Marker's Signature — Rocco

I HAVE CHECKED MY SCORE HOLE BY HOLE.

Competitor's Signature — Tiger Woods

I'm proud of my four-round total when I fought back from an opening front-nine 40. (Augusta National Historic Imagery)

Mom is smiling beautifully while Pop and I embrace behind the eighteenth green. I love the joy on her face. (Bob Martin/Getty Images)

Nick Faldo, the 1996 Masters winner, places the green jacket on me at the awards ceremony. (Timothy A. Clary /Getty Images)

Enjoying the ceremony on the practice green Sunday evening. (Sam Greenwood/Getty Images)

Focused on competing, I hadn't thought through what I would say at the awards ceremony. I spoke from the heart. (Sam Greenwood/Getty Images)

Now this was a surprise: a cake from my housemates to celebrate my win. I've always had a sweet tooth, and it was sweet to dig into this. (Courtesy of Mike Gout)

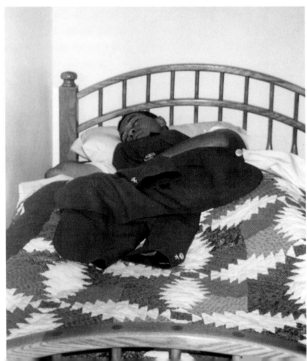

After celebrating Sunday night, I was exhausted, and I had the perfect blanket as I dropped off to sleep. No one was taking the green jacket away from me. (Courtesy of Mrs. Tida Woods)

Tiger Woods

One Erieview Plaza
Suite 1300
Cleveland, Ohio 44114

April 30, 1997

Mr. Jackson T. Stephens
Chairman
Augusta National Golf Club
2604 Washington Road
Augusta, GA 30904

Dear Mr. Stephens:

I would like to take this opprtunity to personally thank you as well as the other officers, members, their committees and the staff of Augusta National Golf Club for the magnificence of the Masters Tournament. What a wonderful and fulfilling experience we golfers, who were fortunate to qualify, had while playing there. This was and always will be a special place for me.

Winning the Masters Tournament was the realization of a lifelong dream, not only for myself, but also for my parents and the black pioneers of golf, who sacrificed so very much so that I could be there. They were all in my thoughts as I proudly slipped on the green jacket as the 1997 Masters champion. The memories of that glorious day will forever be etched in my mind.

I plan to wear the jacket with pride and dignity just as past Masters champions have done, and look forward to returning to Augusta for many years to come. Thank you again for giving me the opportunity to compete not just for myself, but for all minority people of the world.

Sincerely,

Tiger Woods

TW/hlm

My thank-you letter to the club after my win. (Courtesy of Tiger Woods)

Watercolor of Augusta National's stately clubhouse that appears on the front of the menu. (Augusta National Historic Imagery)

I hosted the 1998 Champions Dinner. The Club Menu I chose was straight out of a 22-year-old's playbook, with cheeseburgers, chicken sandwiches, and milk shakes. (Augusta National Historic Imagery)

What an honor to be sitting between Arnold Palmer and Jack Nicklaus, sharing the evening with many of the game's greats at the 1998 Champions Dinner. Arnold will be missed. (Augusta National Historic Imagery)

learn to block out any feeling of insecurity. We had a code word that I could use whenever I thought I couldn't take it anymore. But I never used the code word. I was never going to give in to what he was doing. If I wanted to handle the situations, then I could never give in to him. I had to figure out how to deal with it. I was a quitter if I used the code word. I don't quit. That was how I saw myself. I was starting to get a sense of where I wanted to go in golf, but I also knew that being half black, I had better learn not to let insults penetrate.

Insults are only words, and I couldn't control what anyone said. But I could control how I reacted to what people said. I had to figure that out on my own, with my dad's help. He helped in ways that people thought were hurtful. But I wanted to feel the hurt so that I could overcome it with my golf. My dad taught me how to feel it but not let it affect my game. My mom's Buddhist teachings helped me learn not to let insults get to me. She always advised me to turn the other cheek and to let my golf clubs do the talking.

I thought people who were saying nasty things were fools. Why were they doing that? Did they think they could get to me? They couldn't. I'd been hearing things in tournaments since I was seven or eight years old. People said things to me between green and tee, when they could get close to me. I saw but didn't see. I heard but didn't hear.

My dad deliberately used a lot of profanity when I was hitting balls, all the time, and throughout my swing. "Fuck off, Tiger," he would sometimes say. I didn't mind and even encouraged his cussing, which was poetry. He never repeated himself. He was very, very good at it, and used everything he could possibly use. It was some good stuff, and eventually, I started laughing at it. It was "motherfucker" this, "you little piece of shit," or, "How do you feel being a little nigger?"—things of that nature. That was okay. I was called those things growing up. I heard it at school and in tournaments, and I also knew the feeling of being excluded.

One time Mom gave me money to buy a cold drink at a club, but the club wouldn't serve me. I couldn't change in some locker rooms because I was darker than other kids. I wasn't allowed into their locker rooms, which was an echo of my dad's experiences when he couldn't eat in the same restaurants or stay in the same hotels as his teammates when he played baseball for Kansas State University. He had told me all the stories. In hardening me, he was preparing me for what he believed I might encounter. I was growing up in a much more welcoming and inclusive environment than in his time—he went through the whole civil rights movement, and he knew what that was like. He told me all about it, just like Charlie Sifford did when I met him in Akron, Ohio, where he was living, not long after I turned pro and when I started to think of him as Grandpa Charlie.

But as much improved as race relations were while I was growing up, I could still feel an atmosphere of exclusion when I went into some country clubs or restaurants. By no means am I comparing my experience to what my dad, Grandpa Charlie, and some of the pioneering black golfers such as Ted Rhodes and Lee Elder went through. But something unpleasant was there, and my dad was going to make sure I didn't let it get to me.

Sometimes he talked about what he called "the Look." The Look was comparable to that of somebody walking into a prison with everybody staring at him. Or a white person in an African nation being looked at just because he was the only one who wasn't black. I felt just like they did at some of the clubs. But the thing was, nobody could stop me from playing at the clubs. I could still play the game of golf. Golf has no color barrier when it comes to score, and who wins and who loses. There's no judging. Lowest score wins. I had total control over that.

Grandpa Charlie had knocked down the Caucasian-only clause in the PGA's Constitution. That didn't happen until November 1961, when he was thirty-nine years old. I had read his autobiography, *Just Let Me Play*, and I was horrified by what he had to endure. He told me what it was like. Despite the exclusion and name-calling I had endured, I was grateful I didn't have to deal with the level of racism faced by Charlie and my father. What they had to live through must have required an inner strength that was almost superhuman.

The psychological training that my father used inured me to whatever I might have to deal with in golf. The most important thing I learned was that anybody could say whatever they wanted, but I ultimately had total control over how I reacted. In team sports, if a coach didn't want you to play, you didn't play. My sport, fortunately for me, was based on individual performance. It was the same for Jesse Owens when he won four gold medals in track and field at the 1936 Olympics in Berlin. If he ran faster or jumped farther than anybody else—one medal was in the long jump—he would win. His sport, like mine, has absolutes, and the sports themselves are color-blind. I internalized that sentiment at an early age, which has been foundational for me as a golfer.

My father's approach was what I needed, and it worked for me. Maybe it would be called "tough love" now. It went a long way toward making me the golfer I was becoming as a junior and an amateur, then as I turned pro, and especially when I walked that short distance from the ninth green to the tenth tee after shooting 40. None of this was in my mind right then, but I've been convinced for a long time that had Pop not trained me as he had, I could have easily crumbled after how I started the Masters. I could have panicked, and who knows what would have been going through my mind as I approached the tenth tee and what would prove to be *the* pivotal shot in my still very young professional career?

My dad always said that it was important for me to know what he went through. That was his normality, and I would have mine—there was the Look that I became familiar with. That was normal for me. I was lucky I had golf. I reacted to the Look with silence and the force of my game. Mom talked a lot to me about not reacting any other way. She taught me to internalize anything I was feeling and to find peace from within. I found that peace the most when I was on the course and in tournaments as I moved up the ranks and on to the PGA Tour, especially between the ropes. I felt most at home there; I was in my element and easily slipped into putting walls around myself.

Mom had helped me learn how to drop into a calm state. I'd taken an Intro to Buddhism course in my freshman year at Stanford, but thanks to Mom, I already knew most of the stuff they were teaching. I'd been to Thailand with her three times, most recently in February 1997 to play the Asian Honda Classic in Bangkok, which I won by ten shots. My pals Jerry and Mikey came along. Marko also played in the tournament.

Mom had first taken me there when I was nine and again when I was eighteen. It was important to her, and to me, that I meet some of her family there and get a sense of the Thai culture. I met Mom's father and her grandfather on my first visit. Her father—my grandfather—gave me the Buddha that I have kept in my office for years. He passed away when I was in high school. Back home, we went to our local Buddhist temple every year on my birthday, or as soon as I could get there depending on my schedule. Years later, we still go to the temple. I learned how to meditate there.

After my front nine, I needed to find what Mom called the "quiet spot." It came automatically in that green-to-tee walk. It had become so much a part of me. I did feel cold-blooded, as my dad put it. I could have come apart, but instead I felt in control. The walk was only a few yards, but I accomplished a lot in it. I was ready to play the back nine. I felt centered in a way I hadn't before. I felt tranquil inside. Thinking much later about how much I changed my mental state in that short walk, I thanked Mom and Pop.

Another element played into my mental game after the front nine. Butchie had emphasized that the last shot has nothing to do with the next shot. Just because I hit one bad shot didn't mean I would follow it with another bad shot. Just because I shot 40 didn't mean I would continue to play poorly on the back nine. I was usually angry inside when I hit a bad shot, and sometimes I let it out with my own cuss words or expressions. So what? My dad was always big on getting the bad shot out of my system. If I got pissed off at a bad shot, he and Butchie advised me to let it all out, and in that way to let it go. That was how I would be perfectly clear to play the next shot. If I hadn't done that internally, I'm sure I'd have allowed the anger to fester. By letting it all out, I dissipated the emotion and calmed down so that I could find the quiet spot.

All of this enabled me to step onto the tenth tee in a quiet but determined state of mind. I had all but forgotten that I'd shot 40. It was a new game, and then I hit the two-iron down the tenth fairway. I felt something then and there. The feel produced what I wanted to do with the golf ball, so I told myself to go with it. It was the same feel I had the week prior and for most of my practice before the opening round, even though I was sometimes still unable to stop my hips outrunning my arms. But, with that feel, it was instant correction. I trusted it the rest of the way around the back nine.

After the front nine, I kept telling myself to birdie both par-5s coming in. I figured that the way I was driving the ball, I would have a couple of wedges into the par-4s. If I birdied a couple of the par-4s, that would be four birdies on the back nine, and I'd have gotten back to even par after the front side. That would get me within a hand's reach of the lead. I wouldn't have played myself out of the tournament. All I needed to do was handle the par-5s, make a couple of other birdies, and I would be off to a good start. I kept reminding myself, again and again, that this wasn't that hard. I kept telling Fluff that was the goal. Then I caught a hot streak, and I was hitting the ball on every shot like I had coming into the Masters. I also started putting like I did at Isleworth, improving even on the front nine where my putting had been pretty good.

I was in a flow. After making birdie on ten I

parred eleven and chipped in for birdie on twelve from behind the green. I hit six-iron into the thirteenth, the first of the two par-5s that I told myself I needed to birdie. Two putts later I had the birdie, and was only 1 over for the round with the par-5 fifteenth to play.

After parring fourteen, Nick and I reached the tee on the fifteenth, but we had to wait a few minutes for Paul Stankowski and Steve Stricker to play their second shots. Marko and Ollie got to the tee while we were still waiting. I was sitting on a bench, and Mo sat down beside me. He had been paying attention to how I was doing, and he wasn't impressed. During the delay he asked me what was going on. I answered with one word: "Nothing." He persisted and said that all I needed to do was to pretend I was playing with him, like at Isleworth the week before. He couldn't understand how I was over par, the way I had been playing. He was goosing me a bit, which I didn't mind. I had wondered the same thing while I was playing the front nine.

Finally it was our turn to play. I hit my drive exactly to where Butchie and I had mapped it out to take advantage of the speed bump on the right side of the fairway. The fifteenth was five hundred yards. I left myself 151 yards to the hole and hit a wedge in there. I left myself a four-footer for eagle, which I made. I'd gone from 4 over to 1 under in the space of six holes. I was feeling good now in every part of my game. After another long drive on seventeen I had the eighty-seven yards I've mentioned to the pin, and I hit my sixty-degree wedge to about twelve feet and made that. Two under for the day. My drive on eighteen left me with only ninety-seven yards to the hole. My birdie putt to shoot 29 on the back slid just past the right edge. But 30 was just fine.

I took care of my media obligations, then went to the range with Butchie to work on the same feel I had from the tenth tee through the whole back nine. On the way home, Jerry and Mikey were hungry and wanted to stop at Arby's. We grabbed some food at the drive-thru and continued home. I didn't know this would turn into a nightly ritual for the rest of the week. The boys were superstitious. As long as I was playing well, we were going to stop at Arby's. I didn't argue.

Chapter Seven

Friday, April 11, 1997

Paul Azinger and I were walking side by side up the seventeenth fairway early Friday evening. Our second round was nearly over, and we were chatting away. Paul was even for the round and 3 under for the tournament, while I was 6 under for the day and 8 under through the thirty-four holes I'd played. I was leading the Masters, and I'd played well the second round. My concentration was sharp, and I was hitting plenty of solid shots that came off the clubface just as I wanted. While I didn't want to get distracted—I still had a hole and a half to play—there was no reason we couldn't talk between shots.

Players have different styles, and I had learned how to accommodate. Nick Faldo and I hadn't said a word to each other during the first round, which was fine. He preferred to be locked in every minute and not to step out. I respected that. We got along fine. We shook hands on the eighteenth green, and that was the extent of our interactions.

Paul, on the other hand, was a talker. He and I would do the usual thing of saying "good shot, nice play," that sort of exchange, but we also talked while walking to our shots. People must have wondered what we talked about. Well, surprisingly, we were playing the second round of a major and discussing posture, of all things. Rounds were taking four hours, minimum, as they always did at tournaments, and I was glad to talk about anything and everything. Fluff and I talked about sports—mainly baseball, basketball, and football during the season (I'm a big L.A. Dodgers, L.A. Lakers, and Oakland Raiders fan), and hockey, his favorite sport. He also had quite a repertoire of jokes, and then there was his enduring affection for the Grateful Dead. For me, even the Rolling Stones weren't my music. I went to one concert, heard a couple of songs, and didn't get it. Give me hip-hop anytime.

Compared with the major sports—such as baseball, football, basketball, and hockey—a round of golf on tour takes a long time. Granted, these other sports have gotten longer because of mandated commercial breaks for television, but the only thing that would cause a game to last four hours would be extra innings or overtime.

Although I'd been playing tournaments for a long time, I sometimes still felt worn out mentally, not physically. The time it took to play a tournament round was one of the game's challenges, and I welcomed it. I grinded hard from the first shot to the last putt, so it wasn't surprising that I'd get worn out. It wasn't an issue for me, in the sense that I could grind hard for the four or more likely five hours it took to finish a round. It would have been crazy if I hadn't learned to adjust to how long it took to play.

Golf at the Masters wasn't meant for speed. It was meant to test your resolve and resilience as much, or probably more, than your physical talent. My objective was to give it everything I had for the time I was on the course, for that five-hour window. I had nineteen hours to recover from the mental fatigue. If I couldn't handle the effort, I shouldn't have gone into pro golf.

* * *

It had been a productive round for each of us, although mine hadn't started in a promising way. After a par on one and a long drive into good position on two, I hit a six-iron into the gallery to the right and then dumped my pitch just short of the green. But things looked up quickly when I chipped in. That was my second hole-out in nine holes, and I thought, "Maybe that's a good omen. But then again, maybe it wasn't." I hit driver on the short par-4 third, one of my favorite holes at Augusta or any other course.

It was like the tenth at Riviera in Los Angeles. You could drive the green if you hit a perfect shot. But if you didn't, or tried to get cute with your second, you could easily come up short or go over the green and have an almost impossible shot to get up and down. The green at Riviera is small and on an angle to the drive. The third green at Augusta is also small and protected by severe slopes. The green contours alone could make you queasy, because there are so many sneaky little undulations that you have to consider. I'd heard accounts of, and seen, balls rolling all over the place. You could make eagle or birdie there, and also a bogey or double bogey, just like that. It was a serious golf hole, even if it was only 350 yards.

My plan in using driver was to roll the ball onto the green. If I missed, I wanted the ball on a flat area on the right side. My drive rolled up to that flat portion of the fairway beside the green, which would have given me an easy chip if the ball stopped. But it came back down the slope. Now I had to pitch up and over the slope, otherwise the ball would roll back to me. I hit the pitch firmly enough to carry the slope, but the green on that angle runs away, and it was so firm and fast that I couldn't keep the ball on the green. I chipped back to six feet—the ball just kept rolling—and I missed the par putt. I'd bogeyed a hole that I had nearly reached with my driver.

It was my fault, and I took those ten seconds my father had taught me to use. I let my anger out and got ready to play the par-3 fourth, which I parred with a decent shot to the green and two putts. I was back in that "obsessed with the shot at hand" state—feel the swing, hone in on the target—and proved that to myself when I hit a big drive on the fifth and hit sand wedge to two feet for birdie.

My round proceeded nicely from there, and I felt myself getting on a roll where I was hitting plenty of nice shots and not too many that could hurt me. A long drive on the eighth, which was playing downwind, enabled me to hit a four-iron up the hill and onto the green, where I two-putted for birdie from thirty feet. Nine almost cost me, but I got away with a snap-hooked drive into the trees, and then an intentionally snap-hooked seven-iron toward the green. It didn't hook enough and finished in the gallery to the right of the green.

I was fortunate in that many Augusta spectators plunked their chairs down at the start of a round and never took them away, even if they went to watch golfers on other holes. People were so polite at Augusta that they didn't sit in somebody else's chair. If they did, they would probably have their Masters badges revoked. The badges are so hard to get that nobody wanted to let that happen. Meanwhile, most people stayed in place on the hole they chose. Unlike just about any tournament, the Masters gave players a wall of people that you sometimes chose to use as a backstop.

The people seated to the right of the ninth green definitely provided a backstop for me on my second shot. My ball came out of the trees so hot that it was moving very fast. Who knows where it would have ended up if nobody had been there? My shot ricocheted off somebody sitting there and allowed my ball to end up beside the green. I made par from there to shoot 2 under on the front. I'd gotten to 4 under for the tournament after being 4 over after nine holes.

My round started to really lift off after I began the back nine with pars on the first three holes. I hit three-wood off the tee on the thirteenth and then eight-iron into the green. I had 170 yards for that second shot. I hammered that eight-iron, starting it a bit right. That brought the creek into play, but I was swinging the way I had when I hit that two-iron on ten on Thursday to turn my game around. I was confident that I could draw the ball in over that side of the creek, and if I overdrew it, that wouldn't be a problem. I knew I would have to hammer the eight-iron, and I did. That felt good. The shot finished twenty feet behind the hole. It was a front pin, five yards on.

I had seen that putt before—not because I had it during practice rounds or in the Masters, but because I saw the putt while watching it at Golf Channel studios in Orlando in the months before. I watched how all the putts broke. I wasn't concerned with other shots but fast-forwarded to the putts. I knew from seeing the putt I had for eagle on thirteen that it didn't break as much as I would have otherwise thought. The putt straightened out at the hole. It almost wanted to go to the right, up the hill from where I was putting. You would likely perceive it as going up the ridge, where there was a tier to the right. But I had seen the putt, and read it as flattening out near the hole. I played a little less break than I might have, had I not seen the putt on a previous telecast. I made the putt for eagle and took the lead for the first time. It was satisfying to see that putt work exactly as I thought it would. I've always been thankful to Golf Channel for letting me come in to use its video library. Doing that sure made the difference for that one putt.

Now I was rolling. I hit three-wood, and then sand wedge into fourteen just left of the flag on that wild, topsy-turvy green to one foot, for birdie. My drive on fifteen caught the speed slot again and ran on to just short of the crosswalk, around 350 yards out there. I hit wedge in and made another birdie. I had gone 4 under on thirteen, fourteen, and fifteen. I was hitting short irons into most of the par-4s, and short irons and wedges even into the par-5s.

Nicklaus played the course like this when he won five of his six Masters. He demolished the par-5s and made a lot of birdies on the par-4s because he hit so many wedges into the greens. I read an article in which somebody asked Jack before a round in the 1963 Masters how he was feeling. Jack was twenty-three, and he answered, "Big and young and mean." What a way to feel. Jack knew that he could over-power Augusta if he played his game.

It's hard to overestimate how much of an asset it was to be able to hit the ball miles, and also to hit it high so that you had a chance of having a birdie putt and not always having to putt from forty feet. But Jack also said there wasn't any need to take chances at Augusta, because the course could wreck your scorecard if you made mistakes at holes such as the second, by driving into the trees, or the eleventh, twelfth, thirteenth, fifteenth, and sixteenth because of the water.

I studied how he played the course, and I took his views into account when I thought of how I would play it. Jack had won six Masters, and so I couldn't have a better teacher—even if we hadn't talked very much about how he played the course. But his approach was apparent to me from our one practice round in 1996, and from watching tapes of the Masters he had won.

Another thing I learned from studying Jack was that it was never a good idea to complain about a course. It used to be said that Jack, while sitting in a locker room during a major, heard one player after another coming in and moping about the course. He said to himself, "I'll check that guy off the list of possible winners. And that guy. And that guy." He knew that there was no point in teeing it up if you complained. The course wasn't going to change for you. You had to change for it.

Tom Watson was also a teacher in this regard. He

didn't like links golf when he first played it, because it made no sense to him that one round, into the wind, he might hit a five-iron 130 yards. The next day, downwind, he might hit a five-iron 230 yards. He also didn't like it that the ball bounced all over the place on the firm ground, and often into what are known as "collection" or "gathering" bunkers. But it didn't take long for Tom to appreciate what links golf was all about, and he went on to win five Opens. A bad attitude toward a course gets you nowhere. You might as well not play. But an attitude where you accept the challenge can put you ahead of players in the field who don't.

As for Jack, I learned that he said while I was playing my second round that I made the course into "nothing" because of my length. It was kind of Jack to make such generous comments about me, but I had a long way to go before I could even think of approaching what he had done at the Masters, winning those six times between 1963 and 1986. That was quite a span from start to finish. I was trying to win my first Masters at age twenty-one, a couple of years before Jack's age when he won his first. Jack during his career reached the pinnacle of golf; he *was* the pinnacle. He was fifty-seven when I played the 1997 Masters, and he still had plenty of game even though he wasn't happy with it coming into the tournament. But, as we had seen in 1986, when he was forty-six, he knew how to win once he got himself into contention.

Twelve years later, in 1998, he tied for sixth, four shots behind my buddy Marko, who took the Masters—finally, his first major win. Jack was showing us the value of experience, especially in majors and, maybe more than anywhere else, at Augusta. He was like a detective who had solved the mysteries of the course. I was grateful for what I had learned from him.

* * *

And then there was Arnold. He was sixty-seven and was playing his forty-third straight Masters, having won in 1958, 1960, 1962, and 1964. Arnold had been diagnosed with prostate cancer the previous January and had surgery five days later. The first question he asked his doctor was when he could start playing again, and he was told six weeks. Arnold made a quick calculation and realized that would give him time to prepare for the Masters. If it was at all possible for him to be at Augusta and to play there, you knew he would show up. I was in the locker room with him during one Masters when he was in his seventies, and we started talking about the round ahead of us as we put on our shoes. Conditions were firm, and so we figured it would be a good day because we could both get our drives down the fairways farther. We were talking strategy and kidding around. When I told him he should be able to break 80, he gave me a big "F.U." It was so much fun being with him there, going at one another.

On Friday he was in the first twosome, at 8:20 with Ken Green. I was in the second-to-last twosome with Paul. We had started at 2:39, and so I was getting ready for my round when Arnold came up the eighteenth fairway. He was tired, and he was on his way to shooting 89 to follow his first-round 87. He was given one standing ovation after another during his second round, and the one around the eighteenth green as he approached it and finished his round was loud and prolonged. Arnold and Augusta had been going together for years, and prostate cancer wasn't going to stop him. Arnold said his scores embarrassed him, and that he hadn't thought his compromised health would affect him as much as it did. His scores didn't matter to Arnie's Army.

A few years later, in 2004, Arnold, who was then seventy-four, played his fiftieth and last Masters.

Five years after that, in 2009, Gary Player, then seventy-three, played his fifty-second and last Masters. What other sport can somebody play for half a century?

* * *

My heart rate was elevated as Paul and I walked up the seventeenth fairway, because I had gotten so intense as the round progressed. Fluff's jokes relaxed me, and so did the brief conversations Paul and I had. Now it was time to take my heart rate down, because I was about to play. I was aware of the level I needed my heart rate to be to play shots, when to get jacked up, and when to calm down. There was a certain level I wanted to play at when it came to the energy I needed to put into my swing. I controlled my heart rate through my breathing. I was able to get into an almost meditative state on the course when required.

I parred seventeen and eighteen to shoot 66 and take a three-shot lead over the field. This was a big improvement on the first two times I played the Masters, when I didn't break par in the six rounds I played. One important difference was that I was now a professional golfer, and was playing many more tournaments than when I was in college. I was pulling all-nighters to study for finals at Stanford when I came to Augusta before, which put me at a significant disadvantage playing against the tournament-tough pros. I could hit all the balls I wanted, for hours and hours, and putt on the floor of our volleyball court at Stanford, but there was never a substitute for competition. This time, the tournaments I had played before, and won, suggested I was properly prepared and ready to compete at Augusta.

After my round, I went to the range with Butchie and Fluff to work on my swing. I had hit a couple of iffy shots—like the drive on nine—and I didn't want to leave until I got the shots out of my system and understood what had gone wrong. I worked on moving the ball left to right—a shot I struggled with when I needed to hit it—and was able to do that when I got into a better position with my hands and shaft on the backswing. I hit a couple of bags of balls, and then Jerry drove me home. Well, not home right away. First there was that stop at Arby's, an absolute must now that I'd played well for two straight days.

Going over the round later at the house, hole by hole, I concluded that I had played smart, strategic golf, as I had planned coming into the Masters. It was the style that Nicklaus advocated at Augusta, where he knew so many players would beat themselves by making mental errors and taking unnecessary chances. I wasn't right on it yet, given how young I was, but I'd learned that it was important to play efficient golf. It didn't have to be razzle-dazzle golf, and I didn't need to go at pins that were inaccessible. Jack always said you would have a lot of decent birdie looks if you hit the middle of the greens at Augusta. I tried to do that on most of the holes, except that I enjoyed using the slopes to sometimes take the ball nearer the hole after it landed in a safe spot. I was driving the ball well, so I knew I could take care of the par-5s and make a few birdies on them, or maybe also an eagle or two.

My plan for Saturday was for more of the same. Maybe you could call it boring golf, in that I wasn't forcing things, as I had done in '95 and '96. I was hardly a veteran at Augusta, but I was starting to understand the course and to plot my way around properly. I was doing what I had come to Augusta to do.

Maybe people didn't like it when I said after the second round that I didn't feel different leading at the Masters than I did when I was leading at other tournaments I'd won as a pro. I felt the same because I wasn't playing for the crystal and I wasn't playing for the green jacket, and I wasn't playing to be the first minority golfer to win the Masters. That was all there, but it was background. I was playing for the joy of competition, and for the hunt. But the hunt was to bring out whatever talent I had. The hunt wasn't for a trophy. If I did what I felt I could do, everything else, all those honors and gifts and trophies, would take care of themselves.

Chapter Eight

Saturday, April 12, 1997

If I needed any extra motivation for my third round, Colin Montgomerie provided it during his media conference the day before. Monty was in second place, three shots behind me, and so we were going to play together in the last twosome on Saturday, just after two o'clock. At the conference, Monty was asked about our prospects for Saturday, and he spoke his mind, saying that everybody would see in the third round what I was made of, and that his experience might be a "key factor." There was no question about it: Monty had much more experience. I didn't know Monty at the time, and I came to like him over the years. We've battled quite a bit around the world, and he's been fun to play with. But I took it to heart that neither of us had won a major championship when we went out there on Saturday. And if anything, his comments only strengthened my resolve to play my best golf the rest of the way.

I went through my warm-up routine, and couldn't wait to get to the first tee and into the third round. The last thing Butchie did as we left the range was to remind me of Monty's comments the day before. He could tell Monty might just have sparked something in me. I started par-birdie, and I was fired up. I shot a 4-under 32 on the front side. This was only the third round, but it felt good to be playing so well and increasing my margin not only over Monty but also over the entire field.

I wanted to keep taking care of the par-5s, as I did on the front nine when I birdied the second and eighth holes, and to birdie other holes when opportunities presented themselves. I putted carefully, trying to leave myself tap-ins for pars or birdies on the par-5s that I reached in two. I wanted an easy round that was as stress free as possible. That was nearly impossible at Augusta, though, because of how tricky the greens complexes were. So much thinking and strategy had to go into every approach shot.

The way I played the third hole was a good

example of that. I hit a three-iron off the tee, and then a wedge that went over the green to the right. That was a serious mistake, because I had a brutal pitch back to the hole. Looking at it, you wouldn't think it was that hard. There's the green, and there's the hole, and I have enough room to pinch the ball and put a bit of draw spin on it so that it would catch and sneak on down near the hole to where I'd have a short par putt, or maybe a tap-in. But I didn't spin the ball as much as I wanted to, which annoyed me. I had a hill between me and the hole, and a slope off that hill that went left to right. I was trying to kill the shot with that bit of spin. It would have softened the blow coming into the hill so that it wouldn't have been as hot coming across the crest, and then it would have taken the break to the right and finished near the hole. But it ran on by, because I didn't impart the precise amount of spin that the shot required. The ball ended up running straight, about eight feet by the hole. When I thought about it later, I realized that I did well just to get it there— that's how ticklish the shot was. I made the putt for par, though. I walked to the next tee and told myself, "Okay, that could have been nasty, but you made par. One under after three holes."

I was enjoying the round and Monty's company. He was respectful and complimentary, and would say, "Nice putt, good shot." That's the way golf is supposed to be; I did the same. We had a lot of banter going back and forth, but he knew pretty quickly that he was in a heavyweight battle. He probably also realized that his comments were giving me extra motivation in the round. He was walking with his head down and shoulders slumped. Meanwhile, I kept pushing myself to handle the par-5s and any situations that came up during the round. It didn't hurt that the greens were soft because they had absorbed some rain, so I could attack some pins where I felt that was warranted. The ball was picking up some mud, so I hit some low hooks off the tees to run the ball out and allow the mud to come off.

I was competitive, simple as that. If you challenged me, I wasn't going to back down. Mom knew that, Pop knew that, and that was why they weren't concerned after I shot that 40 on the front nine the first round. They believed in me, and had always told me I could do things on the course that nobody else could do. I'm sure I internalized that self-belief. I didn't believe all the people who were saying and writing that things would be different for me when I turned pro. Why should it be? It was still golf. The ball didn't know I had been a pro for only seven months, and it didn't know I was only twenty-one.

It didn't know I was playing my first Masters as a professional. I'm sure Nicklaus thought this way at the 1986 Masters, when he was forty-six years old. The golf ball didn't know he was forty-six.

Nicklaus rarely received criticism, and for good reason. But he wasn't playing very well when he showed up at the 1986 Masters, and Tom McCollister, a writer for the *Atlanta Journal-Constitution*, and somebody Jack respected, didn't believe he had enough game to win. He wrote an article in the paper the Sunday before Masters week in which he said, "Nicklaus is gone, done. He just doesn't have the game anymore. It's rusted from lack of use. He's forty-six, and nobody that old wins the Masters."

That was true. Nobody that old had won the Masters. But so what? Did it really matter that Nicklaus hadn't won a major in six years, or a PGA Tour event in two years, or that in seven tournaments on tour that year, his best finish was a tie for thirty-ninth? Jack didn't believe any of that mattered. He was coming to Augusta and the Masters, a place and tournament he knew very well, and where he had won the Masters five times. He said at Augusta, "I still want to win and think I can. If nothing else, I'm gonna do it just to show you guys I still can."

It was accurate, though, that he wasn't playing well leading up to the Masters. But Jack Grout, his teacher since he was ten years old, was in his corner. He saw Grout the week before the Masters, and they decided he was using his hands too much in his swing. He needed to get more synchronization between his hands, arms, and body. There were similarities between what he was trying to do at forty-six, and what Butchie and I had worked on since we started together, when I was seventeen.

Jack saw the article that McCollister had written, because a friend staying with him in their rented house had put it on the fridge. Jack couldn't miss it. Then he shot a final-round 65 and won his sixth Masters. It wasn't long after he sat down in the media center that he asked, playfully, "Where's Tom McCollister?" The writer was finishing a story, and he showed up a few minutes later. Nicklaus said, "Hi, Tom...thanks," and McCollister replied, "Glad I could help." Everything was said in good humor, but everybody in Jack's orbit that week knew that the article saying he was finished had given him a shot of motivation.

I enjoyed reading about that Masters, and that incident, as I got older and thought more about playing in the Masters. Then Monty hit me with his comment on the Friday evening before we played. Perfect. Butchie could see it in my eyes as we walked from the range toward the first tee that I was itching to play and to take on the course, Monty, and the rest of the field. But Monty especially.

* * *

I finished the front nine with a two-putt birdie on the eighth and a par on the ninth, to shoot 32. Four under for the front side, and 12 under for the tournament. Forty-five holes of the Masters were over for me, and I was making excellent progress. I wanted to take it as deep as I could, though, without taking any chances or making mistakes. Nicklaus had shot 74, and was talking to the media behind the eighteenth green as I walked from nine to ten. That was the first of a few times we would cross each other's path at a major. I was ready to tee off in the second round of the 2000 U.S. Open at Pebble when a huge roar erupted from the eighteenth green. It was Jack. He had knocked it on the green in two, for the first time in his career. There was a time nobody could hit that green in two, but the ball was going farther and the equipment was more forgiving, and so Jack thought he would give it a go. That was his last U.S. Open.

Two months later, I was playing the PGA Championship at Valhalla in Louisville. I was paired with him for the first two rounds. We were coming up to eighteen in the second round when he said, "Let's finish this correctly," meaning we should each make birdie. He hit his third on the par-5 close to the hole and made birdie, and I also made birdie. During that round, Jack was talking about different generations, and passing the torch. He told me he had played with Gene Sarazen in one of his last majors. And there I was, paired up with Jack in his last PGA. That was a special moment.

* * *

The fairway on the eleventh hole was so wide in 1997 that I could blast my tee shot down the right side. I hit it slightly farther right than I intended, but it didn't matter, because there was room in that area. I had only a nine-iron in, which I hit according to plan: below the hole, leaving me eight feet for birdie. I was pleased to see the ball finish that close to the hole, but it would have been okay with me if it had finished fifteen feet short. The point was to be below the hole. I preferred to have a putt of fifteen feet from below the hole than six feet above the hole. I'd hit a similar shot on the seventh hole, where my sand wedge finished twelve feet below the hole, and I made that for birdie. Below the hole, below the hole, below the hole... That was my theme. This was the only way to score at the Masters. But I didn't have the distance control or the half shots when I had played the Masters twice as an amateur. Butchie and I worked until I got to where I could hit what Fluff called "feeders." I fed the ball toward the hole, using the green's slopes, rather than firing it right at the flag without much distance control. I'd left myself too many putts from above the hole in the '95 and '96 Masters. I sometimes hit a short iron I thought was perfect, but then looked up to see that the ball had carried an extra fifteen yards. Good luck at Augusta with that little distance control.

There were times, though, when it was tough to leave the ball below the hole, sometimes because of the pin position, or because I was hitting a longer club into the green. The greens are at least big enough that you can go at them with a longer club, not that I had that many long irons or fairway woods into even the par-5s.

But on the thirteenth I did. I had 205 yards to carry the water and 236 yards to the hole after hitting three-wood off the tee. The pin was back left, and sitting on a knob. I hit four-iron but bailed out to the left in a swale there. I'd never practiced that shot, not from the downslope in the swale. I'd practiced from the bowl itself, or chipped it from there, but not from the far side. I didn't think I would ever hit the ball there. Many of the spectators who will never get a chance to play the course, and even some of my friends who would later play Augusta with me, couldn't have understood how hard that shot was until they played from there. It was one of those Augusta shots that television can't do justice to. You have to be out there.

I hit such a good little shot there, a little bump spinner, just to get it within ten feet of the hole. But I misread the putt, which didn't help when I hit exactly the putt I wanted, at the inside left. The putt broke left, so I made par. That was one par-5 I didn't take care of, but I felt good about the pitch shot. It was one of the best I had hit on any course, and, as time passed, one of the best I hit at Augusta. But it wasn't the best. Even the pitch and run that I holed from behind the sixteenth green on the last day of the 2005 Masters wasn't the best, as dramatic as it looked with the ball twisting almost ninety degrees after I hit my spot and then dropping into the hole after hesitating a second and looking like it would stop.

The greatest pitch I ever hit at Augusta was one I hit at the sixth hole in the early 2000s, in a Masters that I didn't win. The pin was back left, and I had hit my tee shot way to the back right of the green. I couldn't putt from there because of where the pin was. I had to pitch across a corner of the fringe. I took my sand wedge out because I could put cut spin on it, whereas I couldn't put as much spin with my sixty-degree wedge because of the extra loft. I played a little cut-spin pitch shot from on the green that held up and then rolled down. I left myself on top of the ridge, about four feet from the hole. That was one of the most satisfying pitches I have ever hit at Augusta, probably the best as far as the difficulty of pulling it off. It's not too often that you get to chip off a green at Augusta.

* * *

I did make birdie on the fifteenth, where I pulled my drive and was slightly blocked out by the big tree on the left side. I didn't want to chip a shot down the fairway short of the water, because that leaves a shot that is one of the most treacherous not only at Augusta but also in all of golf. It's sharply downhill, and if I chose that route I could easily spin the ball too much on that kind of a shot. The shot looks easy on television, because the steep slope isn't apparent. You could spin it back into the water, or, trying to make sure you got it on the green, you could hit it over and have a scary shot back up the hill behind the green. That wasn't a shot I wanted.

I had no alternative but to hook a six-iron around the tree. I couldn't aim at the green on that angle, but had to play toward the bunker on the right side. It was a trouble shot, but that was okay. I could really feel a trouble shot, and often hit some of my best shots when I was in recovery mode. The six-iron curved back and finished on the back edge of the green, about thirty-five feet from the hole. Two putts later, I had my birdie. I hadn't birdied the thirteenth, but I had made birdies on three of the par-5s. I was taking care of them, or nearly enough, as was my plan.

After parring fourteen through seventeen, I got to the eighteenth tee 6 under for the day and 14 under for the tournament. The seventeenth was a prime example of a hole where I needed to stick to my game plan, but I could easily have been tempted to take a chance. I had seventy-six yards to the hole after my drive, but the hole was only four yards behind the big, steep bunker on the right front. It wasn't smart to try to leave the ball between the hole and the bunker, because there was so little margin for error. I played well past the hole, took my two-putt par, and moved on. I hit driver off the eighteenth tee, and then sand wedge from 109 yards to the back fringe on the right side. The ball had a lot of spin on it, and it grabbed into the turf and rolled down to within a foot of the hole. I had a clean card, eleven pars and seven birdies, for 65. That was the kind of golf I had been working toward.

Monty and I shook hands on the eighteenth green. His 74 had put him twelve shots behind me, after starting the round three shots behind. He was beaten up but cordial. I liked the way he played, especially because his swing was so repetitive. You could see that, even when he didn't have a good day. Monty hit a cut out there all the time and was one of the best drivers I had played with. He wasn't overly long, and when he didn't cut it as much, and he was feeling good and could turn it over or hit a straight ball, he could get it out there. Otherwise, he went to his slap cut. He didn't miss many fairways.

The media wanted to talk to Monty, and he accepted their invitation, as disappointed in his round as he was. He gave them what they wanted— the straight goods as he saw the situation—just as he had after the second round.

"There is no chance humanly possible that Tiger is going to lose this tournament," Monty said. Somebody mentioned that Norman had lost a six-shot lead the previous year. Monty came up with "This

159

is different. This is very different. Faldo is not lying second for a start [Costantino Rocca was second, nine shots behind me], and Greg Norman is not Tiger Woods." The comment was cutting to Norman, but that was how Monty felt.

My interview lasted quite a while. I was informed of Monty's comments, which I said were kind. But the tournament wasn't over yet, even though I was being asked what size jacket I wore. I didn't know, exactly. Forty-two long, I thought. It was too early to be talking about putting on the green jacket. Sure, I had a big lead, but the tournament was seventy-two holes, not fifty-four. It wasn't over yet. I planned to go home, review my third round, and make some plans for Sunday. I didn't think they would be much different from what they had been for Saturday. I also had something to fall back on, from when I had a six-shot lead going into the last round of the Asian Honda Classic. I played one of my best rounds to that point, and I'd won by ten shots. I planned to think about that Saturday night. It was almost like I was going to hypnotize myself into playing well with a big lead.

Chapter Nine

Sunday, April 13, 1997

This was what I had worked for: a nine-shot lead with one round to go, a situation any golfer would dream of heading into the last round. At the same time, it would be a nightmare to lose such a lead, like Norman had the year before. Losing that big a lead, even though I was still young and relatively inexperienced at Augusta, would follow me the rest of my career. My plan was simple: Make no bogeys and handle the par-5s, and always play the shot so if I miss it, I missed it in the right spot. If I made no bogeys, Costantino would have had to shoot 63 to tie me. If I handled the par-5s and made a couple of birdies, he would have had to shoot 61. Nobody had ever shot 61 in the Masters. Nobody had ever shot 62 at the Masters, or in any major.

I'd read and seen enough about the Masters to

know that it was possible to lose a big lead. The six-shot lead that Greg Norman had lost was the most obvious, but there were also other times a big lead had evaporated. Seve in 1980 had a seven-shot lead going into the last round. No way would he lose that big a lead, or at least that was what everybody assumed. He'd won the Open Championship the year before, and, sure, he had only just turned twenty-three during the Masters, but he was already a superstar. His seven-shot lead increased to ten as he headed into Amen Corner on that Sunday after he shot 33 on the front side. But his lead was only three over the Australian player Jack Newton by the time Seve had finished the thirteenth hole. Crazy things could happen down there in Amen Corner: big numbers, birdies, and eagles that could lead to big shifts on the leaderboard. Seve got himself together and ended up winning by four shots, but it definitely wasn't a walk in the park for him. He was asked what he was thinking after he lost those seven shots, and said, "The fight was on the inside for me. What I say was 'son of beech.'"

Moving forward to the 2016 Masters, look what happened to Jordan Spieth. He was five shots ahead after the front nine the last day, and he then bogeyed the tenth and eleventh holes and made a quad on the twelfth after hitting his tee shot into

Rae's Creek, then took a drop and hit another ball in there. Meanwhile, Danny Willett was birdieing the thirteenth and fourteenth ahead of him. It took all of forty minutes for Spieth to lose eight shots, and eventually Willett won.

Writing from the vantage point of twenty years after I won the 1997 Masters, I see that the lessons of Augusta keep repeating themselves. My dad was right when we spoke that Saturday night. I would have to play an efficient last round and not get caught up in anything except trying to execute my plan. It had been only a year since I had taken a nine-shot lead into the last round of the NCAA Championships at the Honors Course near Chattanooga and shot 80. I still won the individual title by three shots. But 80? I was angry and disappointed in myself.

I knew something about efficiency, having learned a good lesson when I was eleven years old and playing the Optimist Junior World Championship at Mission Bay Golf Course in San Diego. I came up against a kid who was a few inches taller than I was, and he looked strong. He drove the green on the first hole, a short par-4. I had never seen a kid my age hit the ball that far, and it threw me completely off my game. I basically quit after his tee shot, because I felt I couldn't beat him.

When I told my dad what happened later, after he

got home from work, he asked what I made on the first hole. I made par. He asked what the other kid made. He made birdie. I had mentally quit for the round. Right then and there, Pop told me I couldn't control what anyone else did, not in golf and not in life. The only things I could control were my heart, my will, and my effort and my own skill. That was part of being efficient, or, maybe, even ruthless. I then won the Junior World the next year, and I won it in every age bracket after that. If I did fail in a tournament—and I did—that was okay as long as I tried my best. Mom and Dad never made me feel pressure to succeed. My job was to give it everything I had, on every shot. Their constant encouragement and belief in me gave me a quiet, strong confidence that I could not only win, but also dominate.

Nothing changed in my routine. We had gone to Arby's on the way home after the third round, as usual. Then, the night before the final round, I slept really well, getting eight or nine hours. I would usually sleep this well only when I took a lead into the final round of a tournament. My mind was at ease and I had no concerns about my game. There wasn't much to worry about, because I didn't think my swing or concentration would leave me. I knew that anything can go wrong anytime in golf, but that was a distant thought. By the time I went to bed, I had banished the notion from my mind that I could lose a nine-shot lead.

My sleeping patterns had started changing when I went to Stanford, because our team was always on the road. We didn't have matches at home, and Stanford prided itself on putting a semester's load of work into a quarter. There was only one way: to pull all-nighters. I often pulled two or three all-nighters in a row, to try to catch up. I likened it to when somebody was studying to be a doctor and working twenty hours a day during a residency. You have no choice, and you learn not to sleep. I was also competing against people who were smarter than I was—Stanford was full of brilliant students—and they didn't have traveling obligations. How was I going to compete against them? I was traveling to play in college tournaments while still trying to keep up with my studies. We traveled nationally, too, which only made it that much more difficult to keep up. It was another challenge, and I accepted it. I didn't necessarily like it, but I wasn't going to flunk out. Nevertheless, I loved Stanford and I missed it.

* * *

I got to the range my usual hour and twenty minutes ahead of my time, and set up at the far left.

Butchie was there. Fred Couples was at that end, and we joked around while I warmed up. I was eager to get the round started, a round that my dad said the night before at the house would be the hardest one of my life. He was tired after the long week, but he wanted to be sure we had a talk before the last round. He had always been there for me, and he was going to make sure he was at my side the night before I played the final round. I went into his room late at night to check up on him. Everybody had gone to bed.

We were going through the rundown of the tournament through three rounds when he brought up the idea that the last eighteen holes would be the most difficult I had ever faced. He was trying to help me see that it could be hard work to do everything the right way, and not get lackadaisical because of a big lead. I had faced tough competition before, but in match play. If I made a 12 on a hole in match play, it was no big deal. I lost one hole. Who cares? I could come back on the next hole and win that one. Pop told me I had everything to gain, and also everything to lose, and that I should think only about each moment and each shot, and not ahead. Do that, he said, and I would get the job done. He wanted me to go into my world and focus on what I needed to do. I should be myself—and if I could do that, the last round would be one of the most rewarding I had ever played.

My dad knew me so well, and he knew how to say the right thing at the right time. After we lost him in 2006, I missed that the most. I knew him really well, too. We could get on each other and talk about anything we wanted. He had made sure from when I was a kid that he didn't talk down to me, and he went so far as to lean down to my height when I was a little guy, something I do with Sam and Charlie. We planned strategy at tournaments as far back as when I was five years old. There are pictures of me standing on a course with my golf bag on my shoulders, and there's my dad, bending down to speak to me at eye level.

I tried not to think too much about my dad as I prepared mentally for the last round after our talk on Saturday night. Thoughts of him came and went, which was fine. I didn't dwell on them, though. That would have made me too emotional, and I needed to keep my feelings at bay. I needed to do everything I could to give myself the best chance of playing a clinical round of golf—to be that cold-blooded assassin. I could have easily gotten too emotional heading into the last round if I had thought too much about my dad. I wanted to do him and my mom proud, but to do that, I needed to create some emotional distance for Sunday. It wasn't easy, because Pop was not feeling well during the tournament. There were moments when he was himself, but he was out of it for most of the tournament as he drifted off to sleep.

Part of the task I set for myself Sunday was to let thoughts of what was swirling around me drift through my mind. It would have been foolish of me, and not productive, to try to force thoughts out of my mind. My attitude was to let them wash over me. I was asked after my round on Saturday how many times I had closed my eyes and imagined walking up the eighteenth fairway in the lead and with the roar of the crowd. I tried to steer the conversation away from that, and I answered that I focused on playing the holes before eighteen well to set up that walk up the last fairway to the green. But, really, I went much further back as I readied myself for the last round. I thought about the tee shot at the first hole.

Still, thoughts of winning the Masters did flit through my mind, and sometimes for a minute or two. Could this really happen? Was I about to become the youngest golfer to win the Masters? Would winning create opportunities in golf for minorities, as many people were suggesting? What would winning mean to the black golfers before me who had suffered in a world where the color of their skin mattered to people, and in which they didn't have the opportunities I had, not even close? Would winning a golf tournament, even the Masters, really have the social significance that was predicted? The only way we would find out was if I went out and stuck to my game plan and won that green jacket.

I started the final round at 3:08, which has always been right around the time the leader begins. That meant I had played four straight rounds in midafternoon, wire to wire. That's unusual, but Augusta re-paired the players after the first round, and because I'd recovered and shot 70, I was going to be in one of the last half-dozen or so twosomes on Friday. I had a lot of time on my hands every day. I always played very early in pro-ams—usually first off—and if I had my choice, I would have played early in the tournament rounds. But, of course, that's not the way tournament golf worked. If you were playing early on the weekend, you weren't doing well. Playing late left a lot of time. There was no television coverage of the Masters until midafternoon, so it wasn't as if I could see how the guys were doing and maybe get a read on how the course was playing.

Butchie and I made sure, as always, that my last shot on the range was the one I wanted to hit on the first tee. As I was practicing some chipping before the round, I spotted Lee Elder. He had flown up to Atlanta with his wife, Rose, from their home in Florida and then driven to Augusta. He wished me well for the round, and that made me even more determined to take care of business. I had been thinking about Lee and Grandpa Charlie and Ted Rhodes on Saturday night.

Later I learned that Augusta staff members, many of them African-Americans, came out to the oak tree on the lawn near the first tee to watch me start. Other staff members were also there. It was time for me to do something at the Masters that had never been done. The thought crossed my mind as I approached the first tee, and then it slipped away. I had fallen into my bubble of concentration.

I was wearing my red shirt, which I always wore on Sundays in tournaments; a superstition that started with my mom. Red is one of Mom's colors. Every day in Thai tradition is represented by a color, and red is for Sunday. She wanted me to wear it, although I had proven to her that I could win with different colors. When I won a junior tournament while wearing red, Mom said, "See, you play better when you wear red!" During the next tournament I won, I wore blue, but when I wore red I always seemed to win by more strokes. When I got to the '94 U.S. Amateur at Sawgrass, I didn't have any red shirts because I'd forgotten to bring one, so I thought that maybe orange would work in its place. I came from six down in the last match to win. Then, ironically, the colors of the three schools I was looking at, University of Nevada, Las Vegas, Arizona State, and Stanford, were all red. We wore black shorts and red shirts at Stanford. They were our final-day colors. How could I argue with Mom? The red shirt I was wearing in my final round did have some black in it, but that would still work well. Or it was supposed to, anyway.

I could sense the anticipation in the massive gallery as I hit a few putts before going to the first tee. All eyes were on me. I felt a powerful current of support. To many in the gallery, I'm sure I was an object of curiosity, not only because of my skin color, but also because of how I had played for the first three rounds and the lead I had. My comfort level was high as I waited on the first tee for my name to be called.

My first tee shot mirrored my last tee shot on the range. It flew over the bunker on the right side and left me a wedge into the green. I two-putted for par. No stress. No sweat. I took the bunker on two out of play, and hit my drive over that and caught the downslope. That left me an eight-iron into the green. I two-putted for birdie. This was just the start I wanted. Pars on three and four kept me still nine shots ahead of Costantino. It didn't look like he was going to make mistakes. He hit this baby cut out there, what I would call a shrimp little low cut, which was perfect. Every shot was solid, but I had a big enough cushion that I wouldn't allow him to put any heat on me if I kept to my game plan. He couldn't have been more pleasant to play with, giving me complimentary nods and gestures. He didn't speak a lot of English, but his gestures were their own language. I played the Sunday singles match against him later that year in the Ryder Cup, and he spanked me pretty good.

Costantino was a very good player. Golfers remembered when he came to the last hole at the 1995 Open in St Andrews, needing to birdie the hole to get into a play-off against John Daly. His drive came up just short of the green, but he then chunked a long chip shot from the Valley of Sin. The ball came back nearly to his feet, sixty-five feet from the hole. The tournament looked over, but Costantino chose a putter for his third shot and holed it for the birdie he needed. He got down to the ground after the ball fell, pounding the turf in exhilaration. He and Daly went out for the four-hole play-off that is used in the Open. Daly won, but Costantino had come to the golf world's attention.

His reaction to holing the shot that got him into the play-off became part of golfing lore. I couldn't imagine a better guy to have with me in the last twosome at the Masters.

My first bogey in thirty-eight holes came at the fifth, where I hit wedge over the green into the back bunker. The rhythm on my swing was slightly off, and as soon as I hit it, I knew that my approach into the green was going to be long. I had too much speed at the bottom and hit the ball too far. I twisted my body left as soon as I finished my swing, because I knew I'd made a mistake. Maybe I was too fired up. It was a wake-up call, because, while I felt calm, I was also feeding off the adrenaline of leading in the final round. The adrenaline came on the course, never on the range, and so I needed to make sure that Fluff and I were aware of this when we were picking clubs.

Meanwhile, I had very little green to work with, because the hole was cut toward the back of it. I opened up my sixty-degree wedge, and hit a shot that was about as good as I could do from there. But I still left myself ten feet past the hole, and missed that. Costantino made par and picked up a shot. I was eight ahead.

The fairways were lined with spectators, surrounding every green. It had been that way all week, but this time I could sense an air of expectancy. I could hear people saying things like "great playing," and "keep it going," while my ears were almost ringing from people saying "Tiger, Tiger," as I walked up the fairways. I acknowledged them quietly with a tip of my cap, and I tried not to look at anybody directly. It was as if I was looking at a portrait of thousands, where I couldn't make out distinguishing features of any one person. I knew Mom was following every shot, but I didn't see her. She's only about five feet tall, but I doubt I'd have spotted her if she were taller. I also didn't see Phil Knight from Nike, or Lee Elder, who was following me on the front nine. I was looking at a haze of humanity. I saw only the hole I was playing and felt only the shots I had in mind.

The pin was back right on the shelf at the sixth hole. What a great hole. You're way above the green, and spectators you can't see are sitting on the hill below the tee. It was breezy, which made it hard to pick a club. The hole was playing 188 yards. Costantino hit first after his par on the fifth against my bogey, and he came up short and right, and he grunted. He was an expressive golfer. I hit what I thought was a pretty good shot, along a line to the right side of the green. Fluff sensed that it might come up short of the shelf. "Be there, be there," he said, as the ball was in the air. It was there, but not all the way there, and finished just on the fringe. I left myself a thirty-five-foot uphill putt, with the last part being up to the shelf. I two-putted for par, while Costantino bogeyed after coming up eight feet short on his chip shot. I was again nine shots ahead.

But I pulled my two-iron tee shot on the seventh hole into the trees. The trunk of one tree was on a direct line to the green, and other trees meant I couldn't put the ball in the air and try to carry the bunkers in front of the green. I had an opening between a couple of trees, but toward the fairway. Here came a feel shot. Yardage didn't matter. I set my hands ahead of the clubhead, hooded the blade, and hit a low hook that finished in the front middle bunker. I left myself a brutal angle to the hole, and while I hit a good shot over the high lip, it was nearly impossible to get the ball close. I left myself an eight-footer for par and missed that, so now I had bogeyed two of the last three holes. Golf's that way. I thought I was in total control; I felt in command of my game, my emotions, and my thoughts, and then, just like that, things were getting away from me. Costantino parred the seventh, and so I was back to eight shots ahead of him.

I wasn't worried, but I was paying attention. It felt as though the ghost of Norman in '96 was there, but it hadn't gotten close. That helped, or at least I thought it did after I hit a big drive into the middle of the eighth fairway, opposite the bunker and at its far end. I could reach the green from there, and Fluff and I decided a four-iron was the right club. But, just like on my drive on seven, I pulled the shot and it finished in the rough just short of the pine straw and the trees, and about thirty-five yards from the hole. I had a clear shot to the green but had to come over a big hump on my line. The smart shot was a chip and run with my pitching wedge, and it came off exactly as I wanted. The ball ran up the mound and down to the green, about three feet from the hole. It was a hell of a pitch. I was trying to bump the ball over the hill and let gravity take it onto the green. It would bounce left before going up the hill, and then straighten out. I saw that the ball would do a hard right as it got over the hill. I wanted to make sure I got the ball over the hill and then let gravity be my friend. I enjoyed that little shot. The short birdie putt got me back to even for the day, and nine shots clear of Costantino after he parred the hole.

As short as the birdie putt was, it told me I was on my game on the greens. I felt the little hinge in my right hand as the putter neared the ball that I liked, and then I released it. Anybody who was watching my right hand closely could see it load.

The putt was only three feet, but I still had that little bit of hit in my stroke. I had always played with a hit in my stroke, even as a kid. The greens on the public courses I played growing up were kind of slow, so it was important that I had some kind of hit. The greens at Augusta were superfast, but I still wanted that hit. I couldn't putt any other way. The rhythm in my putting was fine, as that three-footer on eight showed me. It was important on Augusta's greens to be decisive, by which I mean you had to pick your line, which would determine your speed, and then ensure there was no breakdown through impact. The putter head had to flow right through the ball, and finish relatively high and directly at the line you picked. That's what happened when I made the three-footer.

My tee shot on the ninth was fifteen yards left of where I wanted it, because the pin was toward the left side of the green, behind the steep bunker at the front left. It was directly between me and the hole, but there was no way I was going to play at the hole. I had ninety yards to the hole, and my target was fifteen feet to the right. I hit my spot and left myself a birdie putt of twelve feet. Over the ball, I took my three practice strokes and then hit the putt. It came up just short, so I had shot even-par 36 on the front nine and taken a nine-shot lead over

Costantino to the back side. My plan was working well, especially considering that I had played the back nine 13 under par in the first three rounds.

* * *

I had played sixty-three holes, and had nine more to go. Fifty-four holes ago, I had stood on the tenth tee 4 over par after shooting that 40 on the opening nine holes. It was three days later now, and I had gone 19 under since then. It had all started during the short walk from the ninth green to the tenth tee on Thursday, when I thought about the way I had swung the club the week before at Isleworth while shooting 59. A lot had changed, but my job wasn't over, not with nine holes to play. I had some thoughts from the ninth green to the tenth tee that were different from what had run through my mind on Thursday, when they were all swing related because I needed to fix whatever had gone wrong.

This time on the walk my mind went to my dad, who was back at the house watching, because he wasn't well enough to follow me around. I thought of Mom, who I knew was walking the whole way around, as she had done for just about every tournament round I had played since I was a little guy. In my mind's eye I saw Lee Elder. Thoughts of Grandpa

Charlie, Ted Rhodes, and everybody who had paved the way for me drifted through my mind. I didn't try to push these thoughts out, because they made me feel good. They were sweet, warm thoughts, and I smiled inside. To the outside, I'm sure I looked extremely focused, and I was. But there was room to enjoy the moment, to appreciate what was happening, and to appreciate the people who had come before me and who had accompanied me on my journey. I thought of the many times my dad had walked along with me, when he was healthy and wanted me to know he was there. He was my protector, and, like Mom, my teacher. There were so many times he was in the gallery watching me, at a small local Southern California tournament, or a U.S. Junior, or a college tournament, or a U.S. Amateur. When he wanted me to know that he was there, to reassure me he was behind me no matter how I did, he called out, "Sam." I knew that was Pop by his distinctive voice. He used the name off the course as well. It always made me smile.

* * *

Just as on the tenth hole Thursday, I chose a two-iron for my tee shot. I had gone back and forth between a two-iron and three-wood in the first three rounds, and I felt I could get to the bottom of the hill because I was swinging well. I felt in balance throughout my swing. But I didn't quite turn the two-iron like I wanted to, so the ball didn't catch the slope in the fairway that would have moved the ball down to the bottom. I left myself 220 yards to the hole, and from there I wanted to leave myself below the hole. I didn't even care how far below the hole. The one thing I didn't want to do was finish past the hole or over the green. I hit a five-iron that finished forty feet short of the hole, which was cut toward the back left of the green—its traditional Sunday position.

I'd seen video of the sixty-foot putt that Ben Crenshaw had made on the tenth green in the last round of the 1984 Masters, to that same pin. Ben started the last round two shots behind Tom Kite, shot 68, and won by two shots over Tom Watson. Ben's an emotional player, and he believed there was a touch of fate in that putt that started him on the way to his first Masters win. He also won in 1995, only a week after his lifelong coach and friend Harvey Penick died. Ben and Tom Kite had been pallbearers at his funeral in Austin, Texas, on the Wednesday before the first round of the Masters. Then he won the Masters, after playing poorly all year. Maybe Bobby Jones was right when he wrote that at some point in a tournament, it seemed destined that one particular player would win.

The putt I faced on the tenth green was a big breaker. I had to start the ball about twelve feet right of the hole, and let the slope feed it back. Even my twenty-one-year-old eyes couldn't see the hole without Fluff attending the flagstick. The putt ran and ran and finished three feet past the hole, which wasn't what I wanted. It was close enough, from that distance, but it was also downhill to the hole. I got down on my haunches, in a baseball catcher's position, framed my eyes on either side with my hands, and examined the putt. This wasn't a putt to take for granted. There isn't such a putt at Augusta. I settled in, took my three practice strokes, shuffled my feet into the ground as I always did, and then forward-pressed to start my stroke. I holed the putt and moved on to the eleventh tee, only a few yards left of the green.

I loved it that the tees and greens were close to one another at Augusta. This was part of what Bobby Jones and Alister MacKenzie wanted to achieve when designing an inland links. The greens and tees at the Old Course, and at links courses everywhere, were so close to one another that a player could sometimes walk off a green and be at the next tee in only a few seconds. This feature of the

Old Course and Augusta National was in its death throes, though. As the ball, and golfers, got longer, the tees on some holes were moved so that it became a trek to get to them.

My tee shot on the eleventh was just what I wanted, long and up the right side. It rolled a long way. The course was drying out after some overnight rain, and I could feel a cold front starting to move in. I had an ideal angle to the pin, which was on the front left of the green only a few paces from the water. The plan was to be right of the hole, that was for sure. This wasn't the time to attack the hole, even though I had only 130 yards in. My wedge finished fifteen feet right of the hole. I rolled the birdie putt in and raised my left hand and putter as the ball dropped. I had a ten-shot lead.

Fluff and I walked the few yards to one of the most intriguing par-3s, and settings, in the game. The patrons—I find it difficult to use that word for the spectators, because it doesn't feel natural— were gathered in the thousands behind the tee. The tee itself seems almost in a fairway. It's simply part of the ground, hardly raised at all. You look from there across Rae's Creek to the twelfth green, and out of the corner of your eye you see the thirteenth tee behind and to the right of the green. Nobody but the players, their caddies, and walking officials go there. You're about to leave a place where many people gather to a place where only a few people go. The change felt surreal to me the first time I experienced it during the '95 Masters, and it's the way I have always felt in that corner of the course.

At the same time, the spectators who collect behind the twelfth tee are like all the people who attend the Masters. There's not another tournament where the spectators are so respectful of the players, or where the silence as you play is so noticeable. The applause was there as I walked to the tee, and it then stopped just like that as I stepped on the tee and got ready to play. I had been given a prolonged standing ovation as soon as I started to walk to the tee, and acknowledged this with assorted smiles, waves, tipping my cap, and then taking it off. I put my tee in the ground and placed the ball on it before standing on the left side, where Fluff and I discussed the shot. The pin was on the far right of the green, over the edge of the bunker. That wasn't close to my target, which was far to the left so that I would take the bunker out of play.

The tee shot at the twelfth is one of the most demanding and confusing in golf, because of the wind and where the green is situated, across Rae's Creek with woods behind. There's so much to the shot. I stood on the tee, checking the wind. It was hard to believe, even after playing in the Masters twice, but it was true that the flags on the eleventh and twelfth greens often looked like they were waving in different directions. Or one would be limp, while the other was moving at a good clip. You couldn't pick a hole where the wind swirled more than the twelfth.

I played there with Davis Love in the final round one year. The flags on the eleventh and twelfth were whipping and the wind was howling. Davis decided to hit six-iron, and to hit a softie to take spin off the shot. He hit the shot and the flag at the green just went *pfft*. It laid down completely. I looked over at the flag on the eleventh, and it was still pumping straight into us. Davis's ball flew over the bunker and up into the bushes behind the green. I was wondering, "Okay, what am I supposed to do?" I pulled out a six-iron and hit a softie myself. All of a sudden I saw the ripples in the water, which meant the wind was back in my face. My ball stalled out and landed just in the front part of the bunker. I was on the downslope, to the back right pin. The tee shot at the twelfth is so tricky. You have to time your swing around the winds, and you have to get lucky.

I aimed at the tongue in the front bunker, planning to hit a straight ball to a draw with my nine-iron. I couldn't cut the nine-iron and get it to the green, which meant I had to hit a draw to get it there. That would take me away from the flag, which would make me miss long and left, or pin-high. That was the shot. I drew it a little more than I wanted to, but I wasn't going to hit a fiddly little eight-iron and try to cut it in there. I wasn't going to mess around with hitting that shot. The idea was to just dump it left, trust my draw, and rely on my lag putting. I picked my spot and hit it. I took some water, and Fluff and I crossed the Hogan Bridge to total peace and quiet. If there's a place in golf that is more of a sanctuary than that area of Augusta National, I've never found it. Back then, standing on the green, while the group ahead played from the thirteenth tee, I could hear the neat sound when a player hit a balata ball out of the middle of a persimmon driver. That's how quiet it was at the twelfth green.

Two putts later I made my par and got out of there. I'd started Amen Corner—the eleventh, twelfth, and thirteenth—with a birdie and a par, and we walked back to the thirteenth tee in the corner of the course. Costantino had played ten, eleven, and twelve 1 over, and so I had picked up another two shots on him. I was up by eleven over him, and, after hitting three-wood, six-iron to the thirteenth, and two-putting for birdie, I was up by twelve. I hit three-wood off the tee again on fourteen, and then hit sand wedge for my second shot. There's a back-board on the back left of the green, which I used. The ball spun back to eight feet. I made that for another birdie. I was 3 under for the round and 18 under for the tournament. There was water on the fifteenth and sixteenth, though, and I didn't want to lose my focus.

Lee Elder had gone into the clubhouse after the front nine, where he watched a few holes. He returned to catch me making birdie on the fourteenth. Jerry had driven my dad to the course when I was playing fifteen. Pop went to the scorer's tent before starting to watch on a television monitor behind the eighteenth green. I was still out there playing, but he was being interviewed. Watching later, it was apparent that he was getting emotional. Pop was asked about what I was doing on the course. He answered, "Truly magnificent. This is a culmination of a lot of hard work, years and years of training, dreams. It's now turned into reality." Asked what he was feeling, Pop answered, "Pride. Pride."

Meanwhile, I was on the fifteenth tee and try-ing to hit a hard draw. It had cooled down quite a lot by then, and so I had put a sweater on—red, of course. I got stuck coming down—my old problem of my hips outracing my arms—and I pushed my drive way right. I hit a four-iron from there, right of right, right even of the right bunker, and I left my third shot short because I couldn't get it on the green from there. I got up and down for par, making a six-footer.

One more hole, the sixteenth, with water to go. My tee shot on the sixteenth left me with a long putt that I had to start at nearly a ninety-degree angle to the hole. It took the curve and finished three feet from the hole. I made that putt, and for the first time I thought, "I'm good from here." I was twelve shots ahead and could win from there. I made par on seventeen and had one more hole to win the Masters. Then, while I was making my swing on the eighteenth tee, a photographer clicked twice on my backswing. I flinched and hooked my tee shot well left of the fairway. I did have more than a few shots to play with, so I wasn't exactly concerned. And my drive was to the left, and not in the trees to the right. I would have a clear shot to the green once the spectators made room for me to hit my second between them.

But where was Fluff? I couldn't see him when I reached my ball. It turned out he was doing his job somewhere out in the fairway, trying to get a yardage for me. He had to be a mathematician to triangulate the distance, because I was so far to the left. But Fluff came up with the number. I'd called his name and jumped up and down to see where he was. The fans had also gotten into it, calling out, "Fluff, Fluff." I was also looking for Costantino to figure out which of us was away and would play first. He was closer to the hole but played first, which was fine with me, and the right thing to do to keep play moving. I had 132 yards to the hole, which was cut behind the bunker on the front left side of the green. Two columns of fans formed leading from my ball toward the green. Lee was near the green. Mom was behind the green with Pop, standing to try to get a view of me after I hit my shot, which finished well up the left side of the green. Pop was smiling and Mom was clapping as I emerged from the crowd, holding my cap high in my right hand with my putter in my left hand. I kept my cap off, and held it and my putter together from the bottom of my left hand, holding it up in the air. Costantino was applauding as I reached the green. Mom was shaking her head, as if to say, "Look at what my son is doing."

I was trying to enjoy the walk up the hill, but I soon saw that I had left my second shot in a bad spot on the green. I didn't even know it was on the green until I got farther up the hill and saw it, because the gallery was in the way as the ball was about to land. The people did applaud as if I had gotten on the green, but I wasn't sure. I knew I had flipped the shot a little left. But then I saw it on the green. It was not an easy putt. I was ticked off for leaving myself a putt that I had never hit before. I was in a trough, and I didn't know what the putt did. I pretty much knew all the breaks on the course, but not that one, because I never thought I'd be there.

Still, Fluff and I were smiling as we got ready for me to hit my putt. Costantino was closer but thoughtfully chose to putt first from thirty feet right of the hole. He putted down to about three feet, but missed that putt. I had two putts to shoot 270 and break the scoring record that Jack Nicklaus had set in the 1965 Masters and that Ray Floyd had tied in the 1976 Masters. I knew about the record, and I wanted to break it. But my focus was on my putt. I hadn't three-putted the entire tournament, and I didn't want to end up by three-putting the last green. The trouble was, I had never seen or practiced the putt I had, and I was looking at the line as I walked to the green and then to my ball. There was one more challenge, to get down in two putts.

I had been playing tournament golf for more than fifteen years, although I was only fifteen months removed from being a teenager. The one thing above all was that I enjoyed the feeling of being on edge. I enjoyed the rush of having everything on the line.

I liked having a putt to win. It was on me. To me, that was fun. If I was playing a seventy-two-hole tournament, it had been a four-round marathon to get to one point, and to have it come down to one shot. What kid hasn't done that on the course or putting green? We had all done that, and now, as professionals, we got to live it. I had the Masters won. That was obvious. But I wanted to get down in two putts. You hate to make a mistake on the last green, no matter how many shots you have in hand.

Three years later I took a ten-shot lead into the last round of the 2000 U.S. Open at Pebble. My goal that day was not to make a bogey. I got into that mind-set of hating to make a bogey, and I was bogey free through the first fifteen holes. The way I played the sixteenth that day at Pebble was another example of my thinking on the eighteenth green at Augusta. At Pebble, as at Augusta, I didn't know what my score was in relation to the other competitors. I knew I was winning, but I could not have cared less at that moment about that. That moment was about not making a bogey, in the same way the moment on the seventy-second green at Augusta was about not three-putting. I was going to get my goal at Augusta, and, three years later, I was going to get it at Pebble. To me, the sixteenth at Pebble was huge. I hit my second over the green from a flier lie in the first cut of rough. I caught a nuker there, a real heater, and missed it long, the only place you couldn't miss it, because the pin was at the back of the green. I was back there in the rough and took a big swing for a shot of only about fifteen yards, trying to undercut it a lot. I didn't realize the ground was hard underneath, and so the face bounced up into the ball and shot it fifteen feet past the hole. I made that right-to-left putt, with a four-inch break. I was seriously pumped after the putt fell, because I was saying to myself the entire time I was reading it, "No bogeys today. I'm not making a bogey today." I parred the hole and parred in to win by fifteen shots. But as much as winning, at least for the moment, I got a big kick out of making that putt and getting through the last round bogey free.

A three-putt on eighteen to finish the Masters was not going to happen. It just wasn't going to happen. The putt was a triple-breaker, maybe a quadruple-breaker. Going off the trough, it started left, and I read it that it would immediately take a quick right after a foot and a half. Looking from my ball down to the hole from the right side of the trough, where my ball was, I confirmed to myself that the little valley there would start kicking it left, and then it would go to the right. It would then come down the hill, and start going more left. There were all these little reads. I got it down there with decent pace, but didn't hit my spot with the first putt, and it didn't move as much right in the middle as I thought.

The five-footer I had for par, and not to three-putt, was nasty because I had to start it outside the hole. It wasn't a hard putt if I could have kept it inside the hole. But I had to convince myself to start that short and fast a putt outside the hole, and to trust my read. I was going to start it outside the hole and make sure I had what I always looked for, cup speed. I had perfect cup speed, and it fell right in the center. I reacted with a right-arm uppercut. I had won by twelve shots and broken the Masters record for the low score in the tournament. Tom Kite shot 70 in the last round and finished second.

Fluff and I embraced on the green, and a minute later my dad and I were hugging and I was crying. I rarely ever cried. But at that moment, I did. My dad had flatlined a few months before. We'd almost lost him. And here he was, with my mom behind the eighteenth green. As we hugged, Pop said, "I love you, and I'm so proud of you."

Those words kept coming back to me for years, and they still do. I keep going back to his words. I will always cherish and never forget the embraces I shared with Pop and Mom behind the eighteenth green, the moment after I won my first Masters. If my dad hadn't given me that putting tip the night before the first round, it wasn't likely that the week would have come off as it did. I made a few putts that opening round, which gave me energy, and then on the back nine I hit some good shots that fed my energy further. Then, suddenly, my putting and the rest of my game came together to produce a magical week. But the week would not have happened if I hadn't putted well.

* * *

After signing my scorecard, I saw Lee Elder and thanked him for his sacrifices and what he meant to the game, how hard he fought to make it to the Masters in 1975. He had to earn a spot, and he did. He became the first black golfer to play the Masters in the year I was born. I had often thought of that.

I was taken to Butler Cabin for the traditional televised ceremony where the defending champion placed the green jacket on the winner's shoulders. It fit well. I wondered how Nick Faldo felt about having to hang around all weekend after missing the cut. But you don't bail out of Augusta for that reason. CBS's lead announcer, Jim Nantz, in the early part of his time hosting the Masters telecast, was there, along with Augusta's vice chairman, Joe

Ford. Nantz asked me what my plan had been for the round, and then mentioned that I was the first African-American, and the first Asian-American, to win the Masters. He asked me what that meant to me, a question that many people had all week—if I won, that is.

I told him that this Masters was all about the black golfers who had come before me, what they had done for me, and that I wasn't a pioneer. They were the pioneers. I told him that, coming up eighteen, I had said a little prayer for them, and said thanks. I also said that I'd been thinking about my dad as I was going into the back nine, and thought to myself, "Let's suck it up. Let's do this."

When I was fourteen, a reporter asked me what was the one tournament that had captured my imagination. I said the Masters, and he asked me why. Sitting in a cart, I answered, "The way blacks have been treated there, [that] they shouldn't be there. And if I win that tournament, it would be really big for us." Only seven years had passed since that interview, and the history of the club—which did run the best and most popular tournament in the world—was always in my mind. I tried to keep that thought as quiet as I could, especially during the Masters.

My objective was to win the tournament, so I had to set aside my feelings about it taking so long for

Augusta to invite a black player to the Masters and to admit black members. I had to play. I couldn't have gone to the first tee and let my mind dwell on these facts. I still had to hit a little fade off the tee, and I still had to post the lowest score. How could I do that if the thoughts swirling at the edges of my mind dug in deeper? I needed to put them in a box, and hit the shots. Walking up eighteen, though, and in the Butler Cabin, I let myself think about the people who had come before me and paved the way for me to play the Masters, and, really, to play at all as a tour pro.

The awards ceremony on the practice green behind the first tee followed the Butler Cabin presentation of the green jacket, which was for television. Faldo again put the jacket on me. Quite a few of Augusta's staff, mostly black people, had left their posts and gathered outside on the lawn and on the verandah on the second floor. In all the years I've been to the Masters since, I have never seen it like that. They wanted to thank me, and I wanted to make sure they knew how thankful I was for their support. Many of them had worked at Augusta for years, and they were part of history. I've won the Masters three more times, but their presence while I spoke on the putting green that first time was significant in a way that couldn't be repeated. A barrier had been broken. I've had many conversations with the staff over the years, and we've exchanged many high fives; it's all the little things that we say and do every year that mean so much to me. The Masters has meant so much to me. It's hard to fathom.

I knew that none of this meant, necessarily, that things would change dramatically for minorities in golf. I hoped that my win would encourage them to play, or to chase their dreams whatever they were. But it would have been naïve of me to think that my win would mean the end of "the Look" when a person from any minority walked into some golf clubs, especially the game's private clubs. I only hoped my win, and how I won, might put a dent in the way others perceived black people.

While speaking on the green during the ceremony, I said that I hadn't thought far enough into the moment to think about what I would say. My next move was to the media center, but I got a call just before I got there. President Bill Clinton was on the line. I took the call in a little room just off the interview area. He knew what the moment was all about, because he said the best thing he saw all day was my father and me embracing behind the eighteenth green. We chatted for a moment, and then I went into the interview room, wearing my green jacket. I said I had never played an entire tournament with my

A game, but that this time, my play had been pretty close. I also said I hoped my win would open some doors for minorities. My biggest hope, though, was that we could one day see one another as people and people alone. I wanted us to be color-blind. Twenty years later, that has yet to happen.

I returned to the Butler Cabin after the press conference so that I could change into a jacket and tie for the dinner that night with Masters officials. Nobody knew what to expect at the dinner. Mom, Jerry, Mikey, Kathy Battaglia and Hughes Norton from IMG, and Dr. Gene McClung, my dad's physician, were there. Jerry had driven Pop back to the house after the round, then returned with the suit and tie that I wore at the dinner. We met at Butler Cabin after I did my interviews. I asked Jerry to try on the jacket, but he said no, that it was mine, and that I won it. But I wanted him to try it on, because I wanted to share the experience.

We left the clubhouse after the dinner. Somebody got our car, and we piled into it, with Jerry driving and Mom in the backseat. After it ended, Augusta quickly became a ghost town. As loud and as big as that sporting event was with the tens of thousands of spectators, it was empty just two or three hours later. They wanted it back to being a club as fast as possible.

We had a CD by the hip-hop group Quad City DJ's, and we put the song "C'Mon N' Ride It (The Train)" on at full blast as we drove down Magnolia Lane to Washington Road, with the windows rolled down in the big Cadillac courtesy car Jerry had driven all week. That song had likely never been played while driving down Magnolia Lane— nor that loudly.

We stopped at Arby's again and continued to the house. Phil Knight was there. He walked the last round, and he was giddy. He was more nervous than Pop. We all made toasts to Pop, and basically told him to get the hell out of there and go to bed, because, one, he shouldn't have even been at the Masters given his condition; and two, he shouldn't be up that late; and three, he wasn't feeling very well and needed the rest; and four, we were about ready to blow the top off every bottle in the house. I wasn't a big drinker, but I was the Masters champion, and everybody was going to town that night.

Later that night, after much celebration, I fell asleep fully clothed and hugging the green jacket like a blanket.

Chapter Ten

Aftermath

I didn't run Monday morning after the last round. But I did fly.

When I woke up the next morning, I wasn't at my best. My head hurt. We flew the short distance to Columbia, South Carolina, where I was going to participate in a charity event. What a crazy day that was. It was an all-day party, and the libations continued. There weren't any ropes on the course, and as I walked around and played, it didn't hit me that I had just won the Masters. I had an obligation to fulfill. I still had to play golf. It started to settle in during the week that I had won, but it didn't set in until a few weeks later that I had won the Masters by twelve shots.

We left from Columbia to go to Cancun for a holiday, something I had planned before the Masters, because I had a sponsorship with Planet Hollywood and its Official All-Star Cafes. The best part of the trip was that I went off the grid there. There weren't any social media then, and I didn't read any newspapers. It was radio silence, which allowed me to get away from all the hoopla. David Letterman and Jay Leno had invited me on their shows, but I chose not to go. I wanted to be with my friends, to hang out on the beach, to eat, drink, and celebrate for three or four days. Until I won, we had planned to go our separate ways, although I would still have gone to Cancun. We decided, the hell with it, we're staying together. We'll keep this thing going for a while— which we did.

We went from Cancun to the Nike offices in Beaverton, Oregon, later in the week, which was where I learned about what had been happening back home. Fuzzy Zoeller had made some comments to CNN at Augusta while I was playing the back nine Sunday. A producer noticed the comments while reviewing the tape. Fuzzy's comments were aired the Sunday after the Masters, on CNN's *Pro Golf Weekly*. They led to quite the reaction.

Here's what Fuzzy said out there on the lawn at Augusta when he was asked about me. "He's doing quite well. Pretty impressive. That little boy is driving well and he's putting well. He's doing everything it takes to win. So, you know what you guys do when he gets in here? You pat him on the back and say congratulations and enjoy it and tell him not to serve fried chicken [at the Champions Dinner that I would host the Tuesday evening of the 1998 Masters] next year. Got it?"

Fuzzy snapped his fingers and walked away from the camera, but then he turned around, and added, "Or collard greens. Or whatever the hell they serve." It bothered me that he turned around and said that. Where did that come from?

I was disappointed in Fuzz, and hurt, when I learned of what he said, especially considering where he made the comments and under what circumstances—when I was on my way to winning the Masters. I also knew that Fuzzy was fast with a quip and liked to joke around. I didn't know him that well, because I was still young in my pro career. But I did know that he made light of everything. I thought he couldn't have meant anything ugly. But at the same time, I wondered why those words had come out of him at that time. His comments had a racist twinge. Would it matter if he meant what he said as a joke? If he had, it sure didn't come across as funny.

What was behind what he said? How could it be that these thoughts were in his mind and that they would come out there, at Augusta? The club itself had always treated me and my family with respect, and so I felt comfortable there. Augusta members were sensitive to accusations of racism in the past. They were getting past that, and the last thing they needed was for the subject to be in the forefront as the Masters that I had just won ended.

I felt both confused and angry, and wasn't sure what to do. Should I respond to Fuzzy? Was it better to leave it alone and not to give his words any power? Why did this kind of incident have to still happen? Why should I allow his words to intrude upon what I had accomplished? My goal all along had been that by playing winning golf I could somehow help golfers, and perhaps people outside the game, be color-blind. Wouldn't that be the best situation to come out of my win, that we could see one another as people and people only? That was a lofty notion, maybe, and even idealistic. But I really thought it could happen, even while I hoped my win would bring more minorities into the game. Maybe I couldn't have it both ways. Maybe I couldn't be seen as a golfer, nothing more, nothing less, while simultaneously hoping more minorities would be drawn to the game.

The whole thing around Fuzzy's comments had taken on a life of its own by the time I found out about it. Kmart, one of his sponsors, dropped him two days after the segment aired. He was getting hateful, malicious threats. I was thinking, "Wow, what is going on here?" I've since gotten to know Fuzzy over the years, and he definitely is funny and lighthearted. Ironically, I played with him in the second round of the '98 Masters. We were hitting balls before our rounds, pretty close to one another. Scott Hoch was trying to be funny when he asked, "Who's going to referee?" We didn't acknowledge him.

Fuzzy's comments didn't come across as right for a lot of people, and I understood their viewpoint. Should he have said that? No. He recognized this quickly, and apologized publicly the Monday after CNN aired his comments.

"My comments were not intended to be racially derogatory," Fuzzy said in a statement, "and I apologize for the fact that they were misconstrued in that fashion. I've been on the tour for twenty-three years, and anybody who knows me knows that I am a jokester. It's too bad that something I said in jest was turned into something it's not, but I didn't mean anything by it and I'm sorry if I offended anybody. If Tiger is offended by it, I apologize to him, too."

I issued a statement a few days later. "At first I was shocked to hear that Fuzzy Zoeller had made these unfortunate remarks," I said. "His attempt at humor was out of bounds, and I was disappointed by it. But having played golf with Fuzzy, I know he is a jokester; and I have concluded that no personal animosity toward me was intended. I respect Fuzzy as a golfer and as a person and for the many good things he has done for others throughout his career. I know he feels badly about his remarks. We all make mistakes, and it is time to move on. I accept Fuzzy's apology and hope everyone can now put this behind us."

I hadn't wanted to issue a statement, because I had done nothing wrong. I'd have preferred to leave it alone, but I was advised to say something. I figured it was all over, but some of the guys on the PGA Tour thought I should have spoken directly to Fuzzy before then. He had tried to call me a couple of times, but I hadn't gotten back to him. I wanted to deal with it in the statement. Maybe I should have been quicker to respond, but I didn't bring on the problem.

Fuzz and I did talk about it one on one when we had lunch at the Colonial the month after I won the Masters. He explained that he wasn't trying to jab at me at all, and that, standing there and talking, he was trying to acknowledge that I had kicked everybody's ass that week. But he said it in an inappropriate, flippant way, and it blew up. He was asked about it for years, it being the sort of incident that could follow somebody for a long time. For me, it was over and done with after our lunch at Colonial.

* * *

On the Tuesday after I won the Masters, the game between the Los Angeles Dodgers and the New York Mets at Shea Stadium was dedicated to Jackie Robinson. He had broken the color barrier in baseball exactly fifty years before at the old Ebbets Field in Brooklyn. He had come up to the majors from the Montreal Royals to play for the then Brooklyn Dodgers. They had played the Boston Braves on that day.

President Clinton had invited me to the ceremony when he called Sunday evening to congratulate me on my Masters win. Robinson's widow, Rachel, was at the ceremony. So were his grandson, along with Sandy Koufax, the filmmaker Spike Lee, and baseball commissioner Bud Selig. I unfortunately had to decline President Clinton's invitation, as I was going on a long-planned vacation—made even better because my pals were now along to celebrate my Masters win.

I took a lot of heat for not attending the ceremony, and it took a while for me to realize I was wrong. I regretted not going, and still do. I should have gone to pay my respects. A few years later, I wrote a letter to Mrs. Robinson, apologizing for my bad decision. Only a few days had passed since I won the Masters, but controversies were taking precedence over my win: the Fuzzy incident, my not attending the game at Shea to help honor Jackie Robinson. Maybe I was only twenty-one, but I realized I had some growing up to do.

* * *

In quiet times on my own after I returned home, I started to appreciate what winning the Masters had done for me. I had won three PGA Tour events before the Masters and gotten into the Tour Championship the previous October. In winning the Masters, though, I got job security. That was the last year in which the winner got a ten-year exemption on the PGA Tour. When Marko won the '98 Masters, he got only a five-year exemption, because the PGA Tour had changed the rule. I was just starting on the PGA Tour, and I was now exempt until I was thirty-one. I had a job for the next decade.

You never know what could happen. Anybody could hit a tree root on a shot and get hurt. You could have an accident, on or off the course, and then you might be off the tour for a year or two. You would have to apply for a medical exemption to get status back.

But to have a job for ten years? That security? That was huge. It was a nice gift, a gift that Mo didn't get. If the Masters winner still got the ten years, he would have been exempt until he was eligible for the Champions Tour. It's not easy to compete in your late forties, so he could have used the ten-year exemption. His five years took him until he was forty-six, which meant he had four years in limbo before he turned fifty. He would have to play a full schedule to make sure he did as well as possible and keep his status. Mo couldn't pick and choose the tournaments to play in. Meanwhile, I got peace of mind from having those ten years. I could take the time required to improve or even change my swing, if I wanted to. And I did want to, even after winning the Masters by twelve shots.

On April 21, eight days after the Masters, I sat down in Chicago for an interview with Oprah Winfrey. It ran two days later. I think I was the only male there. Oprah surprised and shocked me when she read a letter that my dad had written me when I was a child, and it didn't take long for the tears to start running down my face. In the letter, my dad wrote, "I can remember when I taught you that it was okay to cry, and men can cry. It was not a sign of weakness, but a sign of strength." I was not a crier, or I didn't think I was. But the letter got to me, and I didn't mind. I was getting used to it, after having shed some tears when Pop and I embraced eight days before behind the eighteenth green at Augusta.

Oprah and I discussed my heritage, and my wish to call myself Cablinasian. Some friends and I at Stanford were discussing our varied backgrounds one evening when we came up with the term *Cablinasian* for me. I told Oprah, "I'm just who I am, whoever you see in front of you." I didn't think that I was disrespecting blacks by acknowledging my varied ethnicity. To the contrary, I wanted all of us to see one another as human beings, whatever our color and ethnic backgrounds. Without being color-blind, I believed we would be blind to one another. I hoped we could see one another past the identifiers we felt the need to use all the time.

* * *

Butchie and I were watching tapes of the '97 Masters a few weeks later when something about my swing started to bother me. The Byron Nelson tournament in Dallas, where I was going to play for the first time since the Masters, was coming up. I was getting ready. I ended up winning the Nelson, four weeks after the Masters, but I relied on my putting and my short game to do that. My swing felt so out of kilter that I called Butchie after the third round. He noticed some things while watching on television. I thought it would be a good idea to bring him in so that we could work in person. He drove the five hours from his home in Houston on Saturday evening, and we worked together before the last round. I felt more confident on Sunday, but I hadn't made any permanent repairs to what had been going wrong.

While Butchie and I reviewed the Masters tapes, it became apparent to both of us that, while I was swinging well for most of the tournament, I was still too handsy and flashy through the ball. While in the tournament, I felt my swing was solid, and that I had my A game. But that wasn't true, as I began to appreciate. My win had been the result of sixty-three holes of having a functional, timing-based swing, and my timing was as close to perfect as it could be. My putting was also close to perfect. If you combine hitting the ball as long as I was with taking care of the par-5s while having wedges into so many of the greens on the par-4s, with no three-putts for the entire tournament, you're going to do well.

I saw on closer examination that my hands were too active through the ball because I was so far across the line at the top of my swing. The shaft was pointed far right of my target, which forced me to dump my hands a little under coming through, so that I could get the clubface square at impact. I dropped my hands in front of me. I recognized that I had some bad moments, but that I was able to save my mistakes with my hands. It worked for that one week, but I didn't believe it was reliable. I needed a swing that I could trust 100 percent coming down the last hole of a major and needing to hit the right shot. I had done well since turning pro, and my swing had improved considerably since Butchie and I started working together four years before, no doubt about it. My distance control with my short irons was better, although it was still not where I wanted it, while my lag putting had come a long way.

But I needed to improve the position at the top of my swing if I wanted to win on courses that required more control and where the fairways weren't as wide as Augusta's. I'd been proven right about my feeling when I first saw the course in 1995 that Augusta set up perfectly for me. There were also three other majors I wanted to win. I needed to tighten my swing if I was going to have a chance of winning them. Timing took me a long way at Augusta, but I couldn't rely on such timing week in and week out, and in particular, at the U.S. Open, the Open Championship, and the PGA Championship.

I was criticized widely for wanting to change a swing that had won the Masters so decisively. But I didn't care that I had won by twelve shots, or that there was so much criticism. I knew what I needed to do, Butchie knew what I needed to do, and above all, I wanted to do it. I thrived on working on my swing. I was addicted to staying on the range for hours. A typical practice day for me was hitting six hundred balls, working on my short game and putting, playing, sometimes on my own, and working out in the gym for two or three hours. That was the life I wanted. I fed off the crowds at Augusta, and I was grateful for the support I got there, especially on Sunday as Fluff and I walked along. But I would have played the Masters with nobody there and with no hardware on the line.

We went to work. I wore myself out on the range, but I loved working so hard on my swing. I've always enjoyed spending hours and hours on the range, or studying film of my swing. It's been for one objective: to get the most out of myself. I wasn't in the game for the trophies. I was in it to find the answer to one question: How good can I be? I suppose I was searching for perfection, although that's not attainable in golf except for short stretches. I wanted total control of my swing, and, hence, the ball.

It took eighteen months for me to make the swing mine, or to own it, by which I mean that it felt natural and not contrived. I did win the '97 Western Open in July, but it wasn't because I was yet making the swings we were working on—not consistently. I just happened to get some good breaks and to play well enough to win. But I was building my swing and my confidence. I was making so many changes while still trying to play at a high level. I was getting top-ten finishes, but I wanted more stretches of making swings we were trying to implement. I got it for two holes, then four, then nine, then a whole round, then thirty-six holes, and fifty-four, and then an entire tournament. But I didn't win again until the BellSouth in Atlanta in May '98, a period of sixteen PGA Tour events where I told myself every week to stay with what I was doing.

I could see why I was getting hammered for making changes, but I knew my game better than anybody, and I had enough confirmation during practice sessions and on some shots and in some rounds to maintain the belief that I was doing the right thing for the long run.

Finally, as the 1999 season started, I felt I was on it. I'd incorporated the changes, and I went on a tear. I won the PGA Championship that year and seven other tournaments, including six in a row. In 2000, I won the U.S. and British Opens, and the PGA Championship. When I won the 2001 Masters, I had won four straight majors—the Tiger Slam, as people call it—the Grand Slam to me, because I won four majors in a row.

Four years had passed since I won the '97 Masters. I was twenty-five years old, and hungry for more improvements and more wins. I had won six majors, and I wanted more. I thirsted for more, because I loved to compete. I didn't care who it was or what it was. Maybe that was why I got so excited when I was up against Jerry in Ping-Pong or *Mortal Kombat* at our house the week I won my first green jacket. I wanted the rush of competing and the sense of accomplishment. I loved putting mind and body on edge. That to me was fun. That brought me calmness. I felt at peace and the most comfortable when I had to make a shot near the end of a major where I was contending or going to win. It's a very peaceful feeling when you have a chance to win a major championship. In order to get into the position I was in that last round of the '97 Masters, I had to be playing well. Why wouldn't I feel calm? It wasn't like I had been hitting it all over the place, struggling and trying to find my game. I was playing really well. In a major, above all other tournaments, you have been playing really well if you held the lead down the stretch.

* * *

On December 10, 1997, I spent the day with a dozen writers at Bay Hill in Orlando. I'd decided, along with my team, that it would be a good idea for me to get to know some of the main golf writers well, and for them to get to know me. I had made mistakes, of which not attending the Jackie Robinson Day was one. I'd blown off writers after some bad rounds because I didn't see why they needed to speak with me when I'd played lousy. I hoped I would have a long career, and so it seemed like a good idea to spend a day with the writers away from the tournament scene. I was trying to find a balance between the introvert that I was (and still am) and the responsibilities I had to the media and the public at large that were already starting to overwhelm me. I couldn't change my personality—I would never be

Lee Trevino, always talkative, just as he couldn't be me—but maybe I could try to open up, at least in an informal setting such as at Bay Hill.

But during a tournament, forget it. I didn't even like to talk to family or friends the morning of any tournament round. I needed to get into my tournament state—that bubble. I thought again of Greg Norman on the Sunday of the '96 Masters, when he held that six-shot lead over Nick Faldo starting the final round. He said later that he felt fine that morning and went through his usual pre-round routines. But while watching replays of the round, I saw that he looked unsettled, and that he made a series of mistakes. At Bay Hill, I mentioned that the guys who do very well on tour don't talk before a round. They're focused on what they need to do. There's an inner calmness rather than a nervous energy that they need to let out.

Eight months had passed since I won the Masters. I was getting some perspective on what had happened since. I hadn't done much in the U.S. Open, the British Open, and the PGA Championship. I hit a mental wall in early summer, just before the U.S. Open. I had won the Masters, and then the Nelson, and I was in contention at the Colonial in Fort Worth the following week. The Western in July was the last tournament I won that year.

At the same time, my life was changing while I was trying to force it to be the same. I needed to understand what was going on so that I could continue to compete at a high level. I didn't have the mental strength to compete at the U.S. Open, and soon ran out of physical strength. I could feel the intensity draining out of me after playing so many more tournaments than I had played in college. I wasn't going to let that happen again.

* * *

I hosted the Champions Dinner on the Tuesday of the week of the '98 Masters. The menu was up to me, so I decided to serve what any twenty-two-year-old would choose: cheeseburgers, chicken sandwiches, french fries, and milk shakes. Byron Nelson was seated on my right. We were holding knives in our hands and discussing how you hold the club and the grip pressure you apply. Mr. Nelson was talking about how he held it in 1935, and that in 1940 it was different. I was telling him that I had always put a death grip on the club. He slapped me on the knee when I said that. I looked at Mr. Nelson. "Yes?" I laughed. What did he want to tell me? He said, "Keep doing what you're doing."

I loved being at the Champions Dinner. Over

the years, I've noticed that everybody sits in the same spot every dinner. All the International players tend to gather around Gary Player. On my side of the table, it's been Marko and me and Jack and Arnold—we'll miss him at the Champions Dinner—and then you have Freddie and Raymond next to them, and Watson beside them. Fuzzy and Sam Snead were right across from me, and always battled each other for who told the dirtiest joke. They bantered back and forth. Sam usually had the drop-the-mic moment. He outdid most people. When he passed, that torch moved on to Fuzzy. Fuzzy now tells the drop-the-mic joke.

The dinner was open forum the first time I attended, and it's been the same since. Anybody can say anything at any time. Some great stories have been shared that nobody will ever repeat. We've had some arguments, and we've talked about how significant the Masters and Augusta have been in our lives. You then put your green jacket in your locker and don't get it back until you return for the next year's dinner, or if you win that week.

Marko was forty-one when he won the '98 Masters, and it was his first major win. Since we'd met at Isleworth, I had been on him to help him believe that he could still win a major, and I was very happy to put the green jacket on him. He also won the

Open at Royal Birkdale three months later. He told me that he doesn't believe he would have won the '98 Masters had I not pushed him. I felt good when he told me that. Now we can attend every Champions Dinner for the rest of our lives.

I've won the Masters four times, the PGA Championship four times, the Open Championship three times, and the U.S. Open three times. It's hard to believe that I've spent more than half my life at Augusta. I can't imagine that I'll play the Masters as many times as Gary, who played fifty-two, or Arnold, who played fifty. But who knows? I always enjoy driving down Magnolia Lane. Maybe I'll play "C'mon N' Ride It (The Train)" for old times' sake. You never know.

Chapter Eleven

Augusta National's Changes Since 1997

The Augusta National I played in 1997 doesn't play at all like the course now. Everything started to change for the 2002 Masters after club chairman Hootie Johnson decided the course should be lengthened because players were hitting the ball so far due to improvements in equipment, especially the ball. It went from 6,925 yards to 7,210 yards, but that wasn't the only change that influenced the way the course plays. I don't know if the changes—which were done by Tom Fazio, the club's main architectural consultant—were directly attributable to how short the course had played for me five years before; "Tiger-proofing" was the term that was often used.

The course had always been wide since it opened,

because that was how Bobby Jones and Alister MacKenzie wanted it. The objective in driving was to put the ball in the correct places on the fairway to get the best angle into the greens, based on the pin positions. But because of the width of the fairways and the lack of rough, it was never as if a player would feel too anxious off the tees. If you missed a fairway, you could usually find a way to play a running shot from the pine straw; you could find room between what trees there were. Gary Player put it this way, before the 1965 Masters, which Jack Nicklaus won: "All you have to do at Augusta is stand there on the tee and hit the ball at the whole world. You can't get in trouble, the fairways are so wide." Player won the Masters in 1961, 1974, and 1978.

As equipment advanced, Augusta National continued to play shorter for most of the players. Augusta felt it had to do something to make sure we would be hitting similar clubs into the greens that players in the Masters had always used. Augusta wanted to keep the course relevant in the era of the long ball. Hootie said that the club's objective was "to keep this golf course current." I could understand that, although I didn't agree in general with the notion of "Tiger-proofing" the course. The club said that the changes weren't being done because of me alone. Technology was having a real effect on the game.

It was moving faster than the ability of the USGA and the R&A to regulate it. Making the course longer was one thing. It wasn't as easy to understand why Augusta felt it should change the nature of the course in other ways, such as adding rough—that "second cut." It also added trees, which narrowed the corridors of play and eroded the strategic values that Bobby Jones and Alister MacKenzie had created as the course's essential feature. They wanted golfers to play the game by angles, which required wide fairways.

My strategy in 1997 was based on three factors: my length, that the course had no rough, and that it had virtually no trees that would come into play even if I missed fairways. Augusta National was effectively wide open for me. The width— wider than the fairways themselves, because of the absence of rough and the relative absence of trees that impeded progress to the greens—meant that I could join longball golf to strategic golf.

Jones and MacKenzie never meant the course to be penal, but to offer options and make you think. They designed Augusta National to represent strategic golf at its most sophisticated. My length allowed me to take hazards such as bunkers and water out of play for the most part. It also allowed me to use strategy, because of the lack of rough and trees. I planned each round based on my length and where the pins were. I wanted to give myself the most favorable angle to the green based on where the hole was cut. Every player wanted to do this, but my length allowed me to hit shorter clubs in along the angles that I picked, assuming I hit my mark. I averaged 323.1 yards off the tee all week, twenty-five yards longer than the next guy. If I hadn't, well, I still had a shorter shot in without worrying about trees or rough.

All this meant that playing Augusta National in '97 was tremendously enjoyable for me, except during the front nine of the first round. But that was on me, not the course. Going through the holes twenty years later, I can see how much it meant that I could hit the ball a long way. On the first hole, the deep bunker on the right side of the fairway wasn't even there for me. My plan was to hit the drive over the top of the bunker. I didn't see it. If I hit the drive the way I wanted, I had a sand wedge or lob wedge in.

The big bunker on the right side of the second hole didn't exist, either. I'd hit my tee shot right over the bunker, then I'd catch the downslope and have maybe an eight-iron in there for my second shot. On three I hit my drive on the upslope, which—theoretically, anyway—is a simple shot. The bunkers on the fifth weren't where they are now. They were way short of that. I usually hit driver there, and if I hit it solid, I'd be all the way up by the crosswalk. That would be another sand wedge in.

The seventh was only 365 yards, and I wanted to get down there as far as I could to leave myself a sand wedge in. I could hit two-iron and do that. I also hit driver there in 1997, and in 2001, that became my club of choice. Marko convinced me to hit it if I wanted to. If I pulled my drive, or hooked it, I would be up near where you walked off the third tee. That was fine, because I could hit my sand wedge over the pine trees. My length was an advantage not only when I hit my spots, but also when I missed some tee shots right or left. It's hard to overstate how much of an advantage my length was.

Next came the par-5 eighth. I looked forward to playing the hole every round. I saw it as a gift-wrapped birdie and maybe an eagle. The bunker that cuts into the fairway from the right side of the eighth fairway was half the size it is now, and it wasn't an issue for me. I hit my drive over the top of the bunker, and then on nine I hit my tee shot as far as I could and as far right as I could. It was so spacious over there. Every player I had practiced with or talked with advised me to hit it as far right on nine as I could. If that meant into the people, or right of the people, fine. That left me with a perfect angle playing up to the ninth green. I played straight up the hill, directly at the green. No matter where the flag was, it was a pretty easy shot. I got on the left side of the tee box at nine and hit it as hard as I possibly could, and to the right. The front left bunker was not in play from there.

At the tenth, everybody hit their tee shot to about the same spot, because the hole is downhill. Most tee shots landed on the same slope that propelled the ball down the fairway before rolling out. The eleventh was a driver and wedge or sand wedge for me, because the fairway was over a hundred yards wide with no rough and trees on the right side, or at least it seemed that wide to me. The fairway and tree line—for the few trees there were—went all the way to the gallery. Like on nine, I wanted to hit my tee shot as far right as possible. If I got it into the gallery, fine. The only change in my strategy was when the pin was on the right side of the green. I hit my drive to the middle left of the fairway and fired into the green from there. The only issue off the tee was two tree limbs ahead a ways. I was fine if I kept my tee shot under the limbs, or cut it and pounded it up the right side. From there I was looking directly at the green. The water left wasn't in play unless I hit a very poor second.

The strategy at the twelfth, over Rae's Creek, was to put it on the green, anywhere on the green. There's no way I would fiddle with the traditional pin on Sunday, to the right side of the green and behind the bunker. My number there was over on the left side of the green. I didn't even think about the flag. It wasn't there. The twelfth is one of the best par-3s in the world, just the way it is. There's no reason to change it, and I hope Augusta National leaves it alone. It's perfect at 155 yards. The day the hole is lengthened to, oh, two hundred yards will be the day I quit playing the Masters. I'll be done. I can't imagine playing twelve at two hundred yards. We have eight-irons and nine-irons in there, or wedges, six- or seven-irons max, and we still make doubles and triples and worse.

Look at Jordan at the 2016 Masters in the last round. He hit nine-iron into Rae's Creek and made a quad. How often do you make a quad with a nine-iron in your hands?

Then there was Tom Weiskopf. He made a 13 when he put five balls into Rae's Creek during the first round of the 1980 Masters. His tee shot with a seven-iron landed on the fringe of the green and spun back into Rae's Creek. He then hit four more balls into the water from the drop zone twenty yards short of the creek. Tom thought he'd hit his first shot well but that it had too much spin on it. "It was embarrassing," he told reporters after his round. The twelfth can do that to you. You're so exposed. It's some hole.

The thirteenth played short for me in 1997. The tee was to the right of where they moved it a few years later. I hit three-wood or driver at the corner where the fairway turned left. I didn't have to turn the ball at all. It was a straight shot from the tee. The putt I made to take the lead there in the second round doesn't exist anymore because of modifications to the green. The fourteenth was the same, in a sense. I didn't have to turn it much, and a decent drive left me with another wedge into the green.

At the fifteenth I could use those big mounds to the right, the speed slot. I tried to land my drive there, from where the ball would run out down the fairway to where I had eight-iron or less into the green. It was only on Sunday, when I missed my drive, that I had to hit a longer club in, a four-iron. I hit wedge, wedge, and eight-iron the other three rounds. On the seventeenth my intention was to keep my drive left of the big mounds on the right, which would leave me another sand wedge in.

And on the eighteenth, I just kept in mind what Ian Woosnam had done in 1991. He's five foot four, and he took his drive right over the bunkers on the left side of the eighteenth. That stunned me when I first saw it while watching tapes of the Masters. I decided to do the same: hit it over the top of the bunkers. If I missed my tee shot, I didn't want to miss it right because of the forest there. But there was so much room to the left. Fluff and I had a bunch of numbers to the green from that old practice field beyond the bunker and left of the eighteenth fairway. To me, that was fairway, because it was where I wanted to hit my drive, or at least to miss it there if it didn't cut back into the fairway.

The way I saw it, if I drove the ball halfway decently, I would have a lot of wedges into the greens, where short putts had more break then. The lengths of the holes and the distances we hit the ball get all the attention, but changes to the greens are also important. They have more flat spots now, and they aren't nearly as severe as they used to be. The greens in '97 were the only defense if you were coming in with wedges. It made a big difference where the holes were placed. If a hole was cut one step closer to a shelf or a ridge, you weren't left with much of a margin for error. Watching all those old Masters tapes, I hadn't realized the difference a step closer to a shelf or ridge could make. I was like everybody at home. Unless you were at Augusta during the Masters, you didn't have an understanding of the difference.

Augusta really was like an inland links in that way. If you missed a shot by a little, you really missed it by a lot, because the ball could run a long way. Good luck if that happened. But if your shot ran off the green into one of the many swales around the greens, you could at least try to nip it from the tight turf.

The course, at 6,925 yards in 1997, meant a lot of the guys were hitting short irons in. They weren't hitting short irons into the par-5s, and they were hitting sevens and eights into some of the par-4s where I was hitting sand wedges. But they weren't hitting long irons into the greens.

The course played fairly short for most of the guys. Jim Furyk spoke a few years later about the course being fun to play, and that he'd hit shots into what he described as its "crazy" greens. He meant that as a compliment. You had to use your imagination to get near the pins, but you could spin the ball and use the green's contours to do that. Playing there was quite a ride, because you had the chance to play so many different shots. It was a big change from our weekly routine on the PGA Tour of throw the ball in the air and land it right on your number.

It's easy to overuse the word *fun*, but I can't help myself. Augusta National in 1997 was fun, and, I think I'm safe in saying, not only for me.

Then, for the 2002 Masters, they changed the course dramatically. They've changed Augusta National a number of times since it opened, but not so much that you would necessarily notice what they did. But major changes came along for the 2002 Masters. It wasn't as much fun to play the course anymore.

* * *

Until 2002, I didn't go to Augusta before the week of the Masters. The course was pretty much the same, so I didn't feel I needed to see it before the Masters. But Marko and I came up early in 2002 to look at the changes.

Holes one, seven, eight, nine, ten, eleven, thirteen, fourteen, and eighteen were lengthened. All in all, 285 yards were added to the course. (More yardage and trees were added in 2003 and 2006, and the increases continue. The course played 7,435 yards for the 2016 Masters.) We're hitting longer clubs into the greens because of the changes, which was one of the reasons the club has steadily added length. I get that. They're making every carry from the tees longer, and, because of this, shots into the greens are getting longer, for everybody. It's based on our golf ball, which goes too far and doesn't spin nearly as much as the ball we used twenty years ago. It's obvious that the ball is going much farther than it did twenty years ago, or even a few years ago.

I know this just from thinking about the mid-2000s, when we were still using the practice range located on the right side of Magnolia Lane as you drove in to the club. The club had to put in a high fence at the northern boundary of the range, because Washington Road was right there behind it. It had gotten too dangerous for us to hit driver on that range. Under normal conditions, I couldn't carry it over the fence, and neither could Bubba Watson. But I could carry it if I stepped on it. If it was down-wind, out of the south, then I either had to flatten out my drive so it would hit the net, or I'd have to hit a soft one. You couldn't let one go. You could kill somebody driving by on the other side of the fence.

The club eventually put in a new practice area—state of the art, as Augusta does everything—and used only during tournament week. The members use the original range. The pros warm up there when we go in weeks other than the Masters, although the club sometimes allows us to use the tournament range. When we were on the members' range, the club was encouraging us not to hit driver. I hit driver anyway, but I would hit it soft. My ball was bouncing into the fence. I never hit any driver near full, because my three-wood could carry into the net. And this was ten years ago.

Maybe it's that I'm getting older—the 1997 Masters happened half my life ago—but I find myself thinking about what was long then and what is long now. You were long if you carried your driver 280 yards. That was big, if you could carry it that far. Now guys are carrying it 320 yards. It's all about distance today, and Augusta National has followed suit.

Augusta fit my eye better in 1997 than it does now, because I could carry all the bunkers. Nobody carries the bunker on the first hole anymore, or the second hole. Those bunkers are 330 yards out now. Are even the longest hitters going to challenge bunkers that far from the tee? I'd love to see the algorithm that Augusta has. I wonder how they chart every ball, where it lands and how it rolls out. I'd want to know how they manage to laser every shot every player hits in the Masters, where it lands in the fairway and how far it rolls out. Or, if they hit a tree, where it goes from there. Every shot is logged. They have so much information. In 2015, they included climate as a factor. They wanted to understand how far the ball flew in humid conditions, and what the wind was doing when it was humid. The data they've collected, and continue to collect, helps them determine whether they'll lengthen certain holes or not, or flatten slopes like on the first hole.

The course has changed in just about every way imaginable, except for the routing. That's why people say it looks the same year after year. Well, it does, but it doesn't play the same. The players can see the difference. On the first hole, to use that as an example, you either hit your driver alongside or short of the bunker. Sometimes I've hit three-wood, to the left of the bunker or to keep it short of the bunker. It depends on where the tee markers are, and what the wind is doing.

The eleventh is another good example of the effect of adding length—and also, in that case, of moving the tee. The eleventh is 505 yards now, and it plays from a tee that was shifted well right of where it was when I won in '97, when the hole was 455 yards. Now you're hitting out of a chute, and it's become the toughest tee shot on the course. The addition of rough and what is basically a forest to the right of the fairway means the angles that were available aren't there anymore. That takes away the multiple challenges of the hole, by which I mean it's not as interesting a hole because it's become almost a conventional, long par-4. We have enough of those at every course we play.

Augusta National, I believe, has reduced the options that were available. The bump and run from 140 feet that Larry Mize holed on the eleventh hole of the play-off to win the 1987 Masters, for one, is more difficult now. They've raised the right rear side of the green. Augusta was originally designed to force you to create shots around the greens, and so Jones and MacKenzie incorporated mounds everywhere. There's still plenty of slope around and on the greens, but the green's contours aren't as perplexing as they were.

Today's ball is one of the reasons Augusta has made the greens less severe. They've made them easier because we're so much farther back now. But it doesn't matter that we're farther back, because the ball is coming in with less spin. We were using balata balls twenty years ago. The apex of the flight of a balata ball was up, and then it dropped. Today's ball is coming in flatter and hotter, with less spin. The balls aren't stopping, which was why Augusta had to carefully study the ball release patterns for each pin placement.

There's one shot in golf that will never be hit again because the equipment won't allow it. That's Jack's one-iron that he hit on the last hole at Baltusrol in the final round of the 1967 U.S. Open. He had a three-shot lead, drove into the rough, and got it out of there and back to the fairway. Jack was going to win, but he also had a chance to beat Ben Hogan's U.S. Open record with a birdie. He had 237 yards to the hole, and hit this one-iron miles into the sky that came down soft and finished twenty feet from the hole. He made the putt to set the record. I just can't see anybody hitting that shot today, not me, not Jason Day, not Rory McIlroy. The ball doesn't spin enough, first of all. Hitting a one-iron off the ground is almost impossible now, too. And to have it stop on the front part of the green, and the green being elevated, I don't see it. The ball has changed that much. It's also carrying so far that guys were reaching the eighteenth green at Baltusrol during the 2016 PGA Championship with mid-irons.

It probably makes me sound like an old-timer saying things were better back in the day, but I don't see how anybody could say it's a good thing that the ball is going so far, and that it doesn't curve as much because it doesn't spin. Driving the ball accurately used to be more important than now, and I know that because I got myself in plenty of trouble by missing fairways. I had to depend on my recovery game and putting. There's not nearly as much of a demand on precise driving now. Drivers are much more forgiving. If you put today's players on the Augusta National course I played in '97, with the equipment we use today, somebody would go very low. I was hitting drivers and wedges in then, and it played short for me. Today's players are probably thirty yards longer than I was. With so many hitting it so long, somebody would break 60.

Sixty just wouldn't be the barrier it once was. You wouldn't even have to get hot with the putter, because you have so many short irons in there. In '97, you were long if you could hit an eight-iron 150 yards. That's a typical wedge now. My ears still ring when I hear that a guy has 204 yards to the hole, and he's hitting an eight-iron. It doesn't compute, not where I'm coming from.

Imagine Bubba Watson playing the Augusta of '97, and, for example, taking on the bunker from the first tee. He would hit his drive within fifty yards of the green. Or on two, he would hit that cut of his and be down there with a sand wedge in his hand. Look where he drove it on the thirteenth in the last round of the 2014 Masters, which he won. He set up on the right side of the tee, meaning to cut it down the left center of the fairway. But he pushed the shot farther left than he wanted to, and he was anxious for a moment because he didn't know if the ball would carry the trees all along that side. He carried them all right, and left himself a sand wedge into the green. A sand wedge!

Bubba isn't the only one who would have nothing left into the thirteenth green, or other greens. Augusta has over the years tried to add yardage so that we would be hitting the same clubs as before into the greens. We might be hitting the same clubs, but they're going farther. An eight-iron doesn't go 150 yards anymore. Most guys hit an eight-iron 170 yards, and some hit it 180 or longer.

It's a misnomer to say we're hitting the same clubs. It's true that the lofts are jacked up so that an eight-iron is more like the seven-iron, or even six, that we were using twenty years ago. The irons are all delofted. Callaway made all their money early on by jacking up their lofts, and it was the first company to do that. PING jacked up their irons after that, and now it's the same with every manufacturer. We're all hitting our irons longer, but not as much as most golfers would like to believe. We're hitting irons where the lofts aren't the same. As for me, I keep my irons old-school. They're two degrees weaker from what standard is. Rory's wedge is forty-five degrees, or even forty-four. My nine-iron is forty-five degrees. So right there I'm a club off the loft he uses.

All of this bears on what Augusta National has been doing and will need to do to keep guys from going superlow, even into the fifties. They need to consider, and I'm sure they are already considering, what will happen when one of the long-drive guys comes along who can really play, who has the physical and cerebral gifts to understand how to play the game. I'm thinking of somebody who has all the tools to compete at the highest level. You couldn't stop him. All the long hitters nowadays, excluding Rory, are tall. Most of them are at least six feet, and many are six two and above. They're swinging with longer levers. They're accelerating the clubhead over a longer space. Dustin Johnson, Ernie Els, Phil Mickelson, Bubba, they're all six two and taller. Arnold, Jack, and Gary were small compared with the top players now.

When I came on tour, and Phil, Ernie, Vijay Singh, and I were the top four in the world, I was the shortest by far, at six feet. The other guys were six two and above. It's a different game at those heights when you have all the tools. The same thing has happened in basketball. I used to think the power forward Karl Malone was the most ripped-up dude to ever play basketball. College guys today are more ripped than he was. LeBron James looked like that in high school.

Now, winning a golf tournament when it comes down to the last few holes is still more mental than physical. It's about how mentally tough you are, and what you have inside you. But what if a guy has that as well as the physical qualities? That is bound to happen. You can't defend against that. You can do goofy things, like the USGA does in switching up par by changing tees on some holes from one day to the next. I grew up playing the old-school U.S. Opens, where it was the same course every day. The tees were the same every day, all the way back. The fairways were narrow, and the greens were firm if they got dry conditions. They moved the pins around, as happens everywhere. But we knew the tees were always at the back, and that the fairways were about as wide as your finger. Fine. It's the U.S. Open. You have to hit it straight, you have to put the ball in the fairway, and you have to put it on the green. If you miss the fairway, you hack out and from there you have to be damn good from 120 yards in. That was just the way U.S. Opens were, year after year after year.

We didn't play one hole one day as a par-4 and the next as a par-5, which was what happened on eighteen during the 2015 U.S. Open at Chambers Bay. The USGA moved the tees up in the second round and played the hole as a 514-yard par-4. The long hitters could carry their drives over a bunker on the right side. Shorter hitters had to play left of the bunkers into a spot about six yards wide. Jordan Spieth was caught on an open mic Friday saying the eighteenth as a par-4 was the "dumbest hole" he had ever played in his life. The USGA planned to play it as a par-4 again in the last round, but in the end decided not to do that. Maybe they listened to what Jordan said, and it probably also didn't hurt that he said he was contemplating driving up the first fairway if the hole was played as a par-4. Mike Davis, the USGA executive director and the guy who really set up the course, said he made his decision to play it as a par-5 based on forecasted winds out of the west. Jordan birdied the hole, and he won that U.S. Open.

What if Augusta changed par at some of the holes for the Masters? What if they called thirteen a par-4 instead of a par-5? It sounds sacrilegious, but you start thinking this way because of how far the ball is going. Is the thirteenth, one of the most entertaining and challenging risk-reward holes anywhere, really a par-5 if everybody can get to the green with no more than a long iron, and usually something shorter? I hit three-wood, eight-iron into thirteen during the '97 Masters. I hit wedge into fifteen twice, eight-iron once, and on Sunday I hit my drive way right and hit a four-iron right of the green. Thirteen and fifteen weren't really par-5s.

Maybe thirteen should be considered a tremendous, long par-4. Move the tee up a bit and to the right, and call it a par-4. That wouldn't bother me. I'll put it this way. The USGA changed the second hole at Pebble Beach in the 2000 U.S. Open that I won from a par-5 to a par-4 of 484 yards. It was 502 yards and still a par-4 in 2010, when Graeme McDowell won. If they can change Pebble Beach par from 72 to 71, they can change par anywhere. You'd never think a historic site like Pebble Beach would ever change par, but they did.

Sometimes you hear that par is just a number, so who cares if a hole is called a par-4 or a par-5? You hear that a green wasn't designed for a par-4. But it does make a difference in your thinking. It's a mental thing. If a hole is a par-4, you think you don't have an option except to go for the green, whereas if it's a par-5 and you happen to miss your drive, you think it's okay if you lay up and wedge it on and try to make birdie that way. You feel obligated to go for the green when it's a par-4. You almost have to go. The thirteenth at Augusta as a par-4? Bring it on.

Calling a hole a 4 or 5 is different from fooling around with course setups. Jack and I were talking about the ball during the Champions Dinner in

2016. I told Jack I remembered when he was complaining about the Titleist 384 ball being too long, back in the early '80s. He said that was when he started telling the powers-that-be that they needed to rein the ball in. That never happened. No wonder the only guys working television these days are the shorter hitters. You can't last on the PGA Tour unless you're long, or, like Jim Furyk, a supercreative player with a ton of fight.

The game has changed in that the most important club is not the putter. It's the driver. If you lose length, and you're already short to begin with, and you don't hit it straight, you're off the tour. But if you're long, and you have a spell in which you don't hit it straight, you're still long enough to get away with it. Length is much more important than accuracy. Very few short hitters do consistently well. Furyk, of my generation, has been the best player who doesn't hit it very far. He's a rarity. You can't last if you're short. The guys in the booth don't understand the long game, because they've never played it. I don't know any long hitters in the booth. You're forced off the tour if you're short in today's game, and that's a big difference since the '97 Masters.

Augusta over the years has chosen to combat the increased distance by lengthening the course, but that's not the only thing the club has done. I can understand their adding yardage, and that doesn't bother me too much, although I think it's a losing battle until the USGA and the R&A get the ball under control. When I go through the Augusta changes, there are two changes to the actual holes that I wouldn't have done. First are the bunkers they've added up the fairway on the left side of the fifth hole. I don't understand those bunkers. To my eye, they don't fit the course. You can't get to the green from them, not even close. Every other bunker on the course fits, but not those. I've talked to many players and members, and they all feel the same way. I also don't understand why Augusta felt it had to lengthen the seventh hole to 450 yards. It was such a great little par-4 before. Now every par-4 is 440 yards or more, except for the third.

When I look back, I think that Augusta members had to freak out with what I did in '97, with the short clubs I was using into the greens, even the par-5s. I played a game where I could dominate that course. The pins were the only defense they had. They could put the pins on the edges of the greens, dry them out, and get them kind of bluish. That was fine for me, because I had so many wedges in. It gave me an even greater advantage, because I could spread myself out farther from the field if I got hot.

That's not possible now, and not only because I'm

twenty years older and everybody hits it much longer now. The additional length means that the course tests your whole game now. You have to drive it well, and putt and chip well. Augusta was a second-shot course in '97, when you didn't need to drive it that well, especially if you were long. Nobody challenges the bunkers on one, two, or eighteen anymore. You can't carry those bunkers, so you need to think about where you place your drives.

I understand why the club made the changes it did. Augusta National doesn't make the game's rules; that's the responsibility of the USGA and the R&A. There's been some casual discussion about using a ball exclusive to the Masters, but the club has chosen to use more traditional methods at its disposal, such as adding length, rough, sand, and trees. I wish it hadn't come to this. It was always going to be a stretch for me to win eleven green jackets. Meanwhile, the game is now full of bombers who can think and putt. It's difficult to know the right thing to do to counteract how far the ball is going.

I sometimes think about how I would change and set up Augusta for the Masters. The first thing I would do is to get rid of the rough they've added—that second cut—the one right off the fairway. Then I would mow everything down grain, from the tee to the green, instead of the way they do it now. You can see Augusta's whole fleet of mowers, starting to cut the fairways from the green and back to the tee, so that the grain is always into us. The idea is that mowing this way means the ball won't roll out and go that much farther.

I would prefer the grass going down grain throughout the course, as it used to, and I would shave everything down to get the course playing as fast as possible. The course isn't nearly as much an inland links now, not with the cutting of the grain back to us. I would have the grass around the greens supertight, which would bring back the bump-and-run shot. Most of us now throw the ball straight up in the air from around the greens. You see more guys going to more lofted wedges at the Masters. They're putting sixty-two- and sixty-four-degree wedges into their bags, because you have to. The grass is too sticky to play a bump-and-run shot, so the choice is to throw the ball up in the air. The different shots that Raymond, Ollie, and Seve taught me, using anything from a four-iron up, are gone now. You can't hit those shots anymore.

The other thing I would do is cut back the forests on the ninth and eleventh holes to the right of the fairway, and I would put the mounds back on the fifteenth to allow for the speed slot there. The course would be more fun, and that was how Bobby Jones and Alister MacKenzie wanted it to play—a stern challenge for the better player, but fun for everybody. Most of the guys playing the Masters now have never seen it that way. You used to be able to create shots and find a way out of the trees. You could be inventive, because you could find lanes between the trees, and you could also curve the ball more. Augusta was designed to encourage the player to imagine shots and bring them off, the way Seve did. He played the angles. It's not nearly as likely that you can do that today.

I'm sure Augusta National will keep making changes to the course to keep up with technology, but if they ever lengthen twelve, I'm out of there. As I said, I'll have played my last Masters if they play that hole at two hundred yards. Just keep the green firm. That's why Augusta put in the SubAir system under the greens. If there's too much rain, and the greens get soft, the SubAir sucks the moisture out and dries out the greens.

* * *

The more anybody is interested in how Augusta plays today, the more it's evident that the failure of the ruling bodies to regulate the ball has led to changes that should never have happened. Maybe one way for me to express the degree to which the distance the ball goes has affected the game is to reflect not only on Augusta, but also on, say, Seminole Golf Club in Juno Beach, Florida. It's one of the game's classic courses. Donald Ross designed it to be playable for all levels of golfers and, as MacKenzie and Jones did at Augusta, to examine all aspects of the better player's game. Ben Hogan practiced at Seminole before the Masters, because he knew it would be hard and fast tee to green. I wonder what he would think now about the course.

I've played Seminole once and shot 62. I thought, "This is a great course, but what's so challenging about it now?" It's a driver and a wedge every hole today for me. If you shoot 65, you feel you've played poorly. The only challenge today for a tour pro is the speed of the greens. They become extremely slick if you catch them on a day when there's a dry wind out of the north. Otherwise, you bomb it down there, hit your wedge up there tight, and make your birdies. I don't care how fast the greens are, you're always going to keep the ball below the hole if you have wedge in your hands. It's not that difficult.

Bring back persimmon clubs and balata balls, and it's a different deal. Now you're driving it 260 yards, not 330. A couple of the par-4s are driveable with today's equipment. I hit it on the front edge on one par-4, and the member I was with told me that Hogan hit six-iron into the green. Six-iron. I drove it on the front edge, and I'm not even one of the longest hitters.

I was one of the longest hitters in '97, though. Sam Snead and I were talking at the Champions Dinner that I hosted the following year about how far I was hitting it. Sam was giving me hell. Byron Nelson was listening, but he was quiet on the subject. It was apparent that he was as shocked as Sam about the distance I was driving the ball. John Daly had been out on tour for a few years, and he had won two majors and shown what could happen when a guy carried the ball nearly three hundred yards. John was playing a different game. Then I came along. I hit the ball just a bit shorter than John, but I could putt. That was the combo platter. Sam and Byron knew this was the new era. We were playing titanium and metal woods versus their having played persimmon. The game was changing. It was becoming bigger and longer, and they knew it.

* * *

More generally though, golf has become much more of a power game, for men and women on the pro tours. Players don't care about hitting their tee shots into the rough on most courses, because they would rather hit a wedge in from the rough than a longer iron from the fairway. It probably won't be long until we see an eight-thousand-yard course on tour.

Changes in equipment have also made a huge difference. Davis Love and I talked about this when we played a practice round during the 2015 Wyndham Championship in Greensboro. He was the second-to-last player to switch from a persimmon driver to a metal head, which he did for the '97 U.S. Open at Congressional Country Club. I had beaten him in the '96 Las Vegas Invitational, when he used persimmon. Now look at the size of the heads golfers are using; you could probably put three persimmon drivers inside a normal 460cc head.

New, "improved" equipment means plenty of change for players. It wasn't always like this. I once said to Jack Nicklaus that I thought his three-wood used to be his staple, and that he would go to it for a variety of shots. He said he played with it for something like fifteen years, from when he was twenty to when he was thirty-four. He had the same club in his bag. Some players will use the same putter forever, but it's impossible to imagine anybody using any of the other thirteen clubs for fifteen years. The putter I use is basically the same in terms of shape and specs since I was an amateur. I've always used what amounts to a PING Anser 2 putter. That's the putter I used forever as a junior. In college I switched to an Odyssey putter that had the same neck as an Anser 2. Then Scotty Cameron, the master craftsman behind Scotty Cameron putters, created another look-alike Anser 2 for me. I won a lot of tournaments with that, and then I went to a Method putter from Nike. It too was very much like the Anser 2, as is the Scotty I use now. I've effectively used the same putter my entire career.

Sticking with a specific club other than a putter doesn't seem possible, because technology has changed so much. A player has to take advantage of that. Still, I would love it if we played a tournament every year where we had to use a half set. Or play with persimmon and balata on a 6,400-yard course. It would be fun for us to do that a couple of times a year. Low score would still win. The best player that week would still win.

I've talked about equipment, the ball, and design with lots of people in the game; for instance, with Peter Dawson, the longtime R&A secretary, who retired in September 2015; former PGA Tour commissioner Tim Finchem, who retired on January 1, 2017; and the USGA's executive director Mike Davis. There's a prevailing sense that we want to bring more people into the game, and we don't want to frustrate them. Amateur golfers want to use the best equipment out there and to give themselves a higher probability of hitting the ball long, and they want to use irons that are forgiving of mishits. It wouldn't make sense to play equipment that is archaic. But while we want to make the game easier for the amateur, we need to maintain the challenge for the pros.

But how, besides the equipment, do you make the game easier? You keep the heads as big as they are, which helps for distance, and you keep the shafts light, which helps most players swing more easily. They don't fight the shaft. You're giving people the opportunity to get the ball in the air, and to hit it farther. It's a lot more fun to see the ball go farther than to see it spin all over the place and go crazy.

When it comes to design, a business venture I started over ten years ago, you widen landing areas and limit rough height. These are things we can do to keep the game playable for high handicappers and to bring in more people to the game. With smart design, though, you can still set up a course for us pro golfers. It's not hard to do. Just grow the rough four to six inches, and make the fairways twenty yards wide. It wouldn't be fun, but we're tour pros, and if a course has to be eight thousand yards and be set up like that, well, that's a shame but that's the way the game has gone.

My focus is on designing fun and playable golf courses; golf isn't only about tour pros, after all. We create the wide landing areas off the tee and often clear areas outside of the fairway, making it difficult for golfers to lose balls. We design multiple options to reach the green, including options to bounce the ball up. By limiting rough around the greens, we give players a lot of options for recovery shots, including the use of a putter. I want golfers to be able to use the ground, and I have since my first exposure to links golf in the mid-1990s.

We've also designed a couple of short courses as part of the practice facilities, with par-3s ranging from about thirty to 140 yards. This is important to me, and so I've incorporated such courses at Diamante in Cabo San Lucas and Bluejack National outside of Houston. I look at these courses not as add-ons but as integral parts of the clubs. The name of the short course at Bluejack National says exactly what I want to create; it's ten holes, and it's called the Playgrounds. These short courses are the perfect places for kids and even adults to be introduced to the game, for families and friends to come together, and for experienced players to hone their skills. They're also a great option for someone short on time.

I got a big kick out of the first hole when we opened the Playgrounds in March 2016. The video of twelve-year-old Taylor Crozier getting a hole in one went viral. There's almost nothing in golf more exciting than getting a hole in one, and a golfer has ten chances on the Playgrounds. That means ten opportunities to get extra jazzed up about the game. Bluejack is already being recognized for its design; *Golf Magazine* and *Golf Digest* named it the best new private course for 2016 in the United States. I feel good about that, because it means my design concept is being accepted.

On the other side of the scale, I haven't had the opportunity to design a championship course yet. If I did, the design would be based on topography, what I was given to work with, and on angles. I enjoy playing the Australian Sandbelt courses in Melbourne. Those courses don't need a 240-yard par-3 to be hard. The seventh hole at Royal Melbourne is only 150 yards, but it's the scariest 150 yards you'll ever see. I'm on the tee and wondering whether I can hit the ball on the green, and if I don't, whether I can get it up and down. And I have a wedge in my hands. You would much rather be hitting into the wind than downwind, because you have a backboard. The same thing goes for the twelfth at Augusta. I'd much rather hit into the wind there. If the green is firm, it's a frightening shot at 155 yards.

And yet, some really long par-3s do make sense. The eighth at Oakmont in the 2016 U.S. Open played 299 yards the last day, but it was designed to be long. The hole is wide open at the front, where the fairway is fifty to sixty yards. It's not a matter of carrying your tee shot 250 yards to a little spot. That doesn't make sense to me. I wouldn't design a hole like that. But the eighth at Oakmont works.

I didn't play the 2016 U.S. Open, but I did play that hole in the 2007 U.S. Open when it was around 280 yards. It was really quirky playing it at that distance, but we didn't mind. I could stripe my shot out to the right and putt from twenty yards off the green, or chip it, or I could get to the front edge and putt it. I wasn't going to make birdie there, but it was easy to make par, and the worst I would make was 4.

I think a lot about course conditioning as it concerns playability. I would like to see more courses firm and fast. That to me is a test, because the player has to think about what the hell the ball is going to do on the ground after a tee shot. That's much more interesting than just hitting driver up in the air, and the ball rolls out five or six feet. Then you have a wedge or a nine-iron or whatever in there, and you hit the shot and plunk. It stays right where it lands. But you have to think harder if you have spring in the ground. Am I going to take on this corner, because my ball will be in the rough on the other side if I don't go around the corner? But if the greens are hard and fast, I can't spin the ball from the rough. I'll be dead. I'll have to play back to the fairway. And if I play back, that makes the course longer.

One big challenge is to try to design a course for amateurs and for tour pros, without making the holes so different from one another. You need angles. The farther a guy hits his drive on fairways that have angles, the harder it is to hit the fairways. If Fred Funk hits a drive on the same line as Jason Day—except for a dead straight ball—he's going to be in the fairway while Jason is on the other side of the gallery. Pete Dye is one architect who pays attention to angles. He gives you all these different tees, so that the farther back you go, the more angled the fairway becomes. You're playing more doglegs from farther back, but the more up you go, the straighter it is. You're adding length by creating angles.

The big problem is that guys are hitting the ball so far that we need length unless a course is playing superfirm and fast, like the Australian Sandbelt courses usually do. Then you can get away with playing a shorter course for tournaments. The ball can roll into the rough on either side of the fairway, which makes the course narrow. Because it's so fast, we can play a course like Royal Melbourne in a championship. But the challenge is destroyed if the course plays soft. We would shoot 20-plus under par. Maybe that's okay, though. The R&A doesn't care about the winning score at the Open. Conditions dictate the score. They've lengthened the Open courses, but they don't go in for tricking them up.

Equipment isn't the only thing that's changed the game since the '97 Masters. There's so much new technology. I use a Full Swing Golf simulator at home and find it very helpful. I can play PGA Tour courses and I can set conditions to be firm or soft, on the fairways and greens. The data available tell me if I'm getting where I want to with my swing. I can find out about my launch angle, spin rate, ball speed, spin axis, face-to-path ratio, and much more. The information helps me dial in my equipment as well.

Launch monitors are also useful tools, and many players take one with them on tour, because you can set it on the range and check data similar to what the Full Swing Golf simulator provides indoors. I'm sure I would have found it easier to change my swing after the '97 Masters if one had been available then. I didn't know what my numbers were. It would have helped me get to the changes I wanted to make more quickly.

There's a downside to launch monitors, though, and you see it all the time on tour. Players use them while hitting balls from flat lies on the range, and there's no adrenaline surging through their bodies. If you're looking for exact numbers on how far you hit your irons, it's the wrong way to go about it. You could be flying high as a kite in a tournament. Your heart's pumping and racing, so you're going to hit the ball farther, sometimes a club farther.

I didn't have a launch monitor in 1997, but I did have access to video technology and could slow down images to see swing positions I needed to change. I think sometimes of how Ben Hogan would have fared if he had access to the technology that has become available since he played. It probably would have been much easier for him to change his swing if he had a video camera, let alone a launch monitor.

Even video might be a mixed bag, though. I was in Korea once for a Nike day, and watched a little girl who had the most beautiful swing. I asked her how long she had been playing, and she told me a year. I said, really, your swing is very good. Then I asked her what she normally shoots. She said she had never played a course. She learned her swing from watching YouTube. She knew how to swing, and she loved the hitting bay. She had no idea how to play the game, but she sure did know how to swing.

I work on technique all the time, and I use whatever technology I find useful. I'll hit balls on the range into a three-yard maximum gap for each club, assuming there's no wind. Add adrenaline to my system in a tournament, put a club in my hands, and I can hit it ten yards farther. It's hard to duplicate that on the range. That's where players get into trouble with technology. But it's nice to understand what the club is doing, what the face is doing, your attack angle, and your swing plane. Knowing these elements is advantageous, but it's not going to help get you out of the trees.

Launch monitors, relied on too much, can be dangerous in that they can move players away from trusting their golfing sense. Nobody gets to the pro tours without having a ton of natural talent and a deep feel for the game and the shots any round can present. We can get into trouble, and so can any amateur golfer, by relying too much on outside agencies. A good example is when a caddie lines up a player on the fairway or especially on the green. This should be outlawed. It's the responsibility of players to line themselves up. LPGA players use their caddies to line them up all the time, and it's creeping into the men's game. The worst is when a caddie lines up a player on a twenty-foot putt. To me, that's ridiculous. How do you know whether your putter blade is lined up a degree or two off, and that you're going to return your putter blade to exactly that spot? I mean, come on!

Golfers who win, and win frequently, trust their intuition. Eleven years after the '97 Masters, when I won that 2008 U.S. Open—my fourteenth and most recent major—in a play-off over Rocco Mediate, I had a fifteen-foot putt on the last hole of regulation play to tie him. The green was far from Augusta-smooth. The ball was going to bounce. Only one of two things could happen. I'd make the putt, or I'd miss it. I made sure the face of my putter contacted the ball at its midpoint, from my hitting up on the putt. I also meant to hook the putt slightly. I made those decisions to counteract as much as possible the conditions on the green. Still, the ball bounced, as is apparent from the video of the putt. The putt went in. I had the same feeling over that putt as I had over the five-footer on the last hole of the '97 Masters. That ball was going down.

Postscript

And so...

As I look back, at the age of forty-one, at my first Masters win, much has happened since that memorable Sunday in April 1997. At twenty-one, I didn't really think about having kids. My daughter, Sam, born 2007, and son, Charlie, born 2009, are the lights of my life. The closeness we share brings me the greatest pleasure.

Their mother, Elin Nordegren, and I were so much in love when we married in 2004. But I betrayed her. My dishonesty and selfishness caused her intense pain. Elin and I tried to repair the damage I had done, but we couldn't. My regret will last a lifetime. Still, Elin and I are devoted to our kids, and we have become best friends as we care for them. It's all about the kids for us.

Along with moving into middle age, for me comes an even deeper appreciation for how much my parents have meant in my life. Being a father makes me think about my dad even more. He taught and inspired me and helped me gain confidence in myself so that I could go out into the world—fly on my own, and to learn from mistakes. I hope to help my children do the same. I can't imagine any feeling more satisfying than seeing my kids happy—whatever they choose to do.

My mother, meanwhile, has always been a strong and loving presence in my life. She lives a few minutes away from me in Jupiter in a house that she designed, a home where she has a room for Sam and a room for Charlie. She loves her grandkids so much. She's always thinking family, and she never wavers in her support. We have had many heart-to-heart talks.

At the same time, I miss my talks with my father. I miss his counsel and his courage. I miss him every day, in oh so many ways. Pop died on May 3, 2006, and not a day goes by that I don't think about him. He too would have been disappointed in my poor personal decisions. His influence on me was far-reaching and it continues. I didn't need to be reminded of how profound an influence he has had, but I did need to take some time off after he died.

I hadn't competed since the Masters in April 2006, where I finished three shots behind Phil Mickelson and realized I had done something that Pop would never have approved of. I had played for somebody else—in this case, for him. Pop had always told me to play only for myself. I learned a lesson, thanks, as always, to him. The lesson was simple: I should play only for myself.

I returned to play the U.S. Open six weeks after Pop died. In the time between his death and the U.S. Open, I received messages of support from people all over the world, which touched me. I thought I was ready to tee it up again, but it was obvious that I wasn't, and I missed the cut. That was the first time I'd missed the cut in thirty-seven majors as a professional. I played again three weeks later at the Western Open in Chicago, and tied for second.

Then I won the Open Championship two weeks later at Hoylake in Liverpool. I broke down in tears as soon as I holed out on the last green. That was unlike me, but it showed me again how much I missed my dad. I knew that he would have been proud of how I thought my way around Hoylake, which was bone-dry. I hit a driver once all week, because my goal was to stay short of the pot bunkers. I didn't care if I had a longer club into the greens. On the fourteenth hole in the second round,

I hit a two-iron off the tee and then holed a four-iron for an eagle. Golf is so much a game of strategy and of imposing your will upon every shot. I did that, and then my emotions came pouring out, just as they had when I won the '97 Masters.

Every time I play the Masters, I envision Pop and me embracing behind the eighteenth green after I putted out. Pop would have loved being a grandfather to Sam and Charlie. Elin and I named Sam to honor him. As I've mentioned, he used to call me Sam whenever he wanted me to know he was there while I was playing—or, for that matter, anywhere. We thought of Samantha instead of Sam, but that wouldn't have properly honored my dad. Charlie is named after Grandpa Charlie Sifford. If he hadn't been as brave as he was, struggling to break the PGA's Caucasian-only clause, there might not have been a place for me in pro golf. I would therefore never have met Elin, and Sam and Charlie would never have been born.

Grandpa Charlie died on February 3, 2015, and I often think how fortunate I was to get to know him, and what he had been through and overcome. I thought of him as my adopted grandpa, and he thought of me as his adopted grandson. He was proud of my accomplishments, and he was a constant source of encouragement to me. His example helped me deal with any obstacles I faced.

When it comes to my accomplishments on the course, Pop once predicted I would win fourteen majors, and, as I write in early 2017, that's where I am. I have no idea why he came up with that figure, but I know he would have encouraged me to continue to try to win more—if I wanted to put in the time and effort.

I've had many well-documented injuries. In between 1994 and 2016, I went though four knee surgeries and three back surgeries, along with other procedures. I probably came back too early from some of the surgeries, but I was single-minded in my desire to compete and my need for competition. I pushed hard, maybe too hard sometimes.

Then again, had I not pushed hard, I wouldn't have won the Masters in 1997, nor would I have won the 2008 U.S. Open. During that event, I went down to the ground many times during the tournament because of two stress fractures in my left tibia, and the lack of an ACL in my left knee. I'd ruptured the ACL while running. But I could play because the pain would come after I hit the ball. It didn't lessen the pain, but I could at least swing the way I wanted to. While it's in the nature of athletes to push through their pain, it might have been smart for me to be more cautious.

It became difficult for me to make the swings I wanted after my back surgeries. The first, in 2014, kept me out of the Masters that year. The back pain necessitating that surgery came during my back-swing as I turned behind the ball. But I chose to ignore it and swing through the ball. Did my relentless desire to keep going, no matter how much I was hurting, contribute to more physical problems? I don't know, but I again chose to push hard.

I've paid a price. I had my second back surgery in September 2015, and a follow-up procedure in the same area of my back a few weeks later. This time I wasn't going to return to competition too early. I ended up taking more than a year off. I missed competing, but, finally, I had taken the advice my doctors gave me.

This doesn't mean that I regret my decision to keep going hard. I can live with the choices I made. I made many swing changes to improve and to compensate for my injuries. I worked out because I enjoyed it and because I believed it would only make me stronger physically and mentally.

As pleased as I am at my tournament record, I am also proud of what I've accomplished off the course.

When my dad and I started the Tiger Woods Foundation after I turned pro, we looked at it mostly as a way to introduce inner-city kids and minorities to golf. Typically, I would do a clinic at a public course during a tournament, as I did during the '97 Masters.

What none of us could see coming were the 9/11 attacks in 2001. Along with the horror came resolve for many people, including me. That week the WGC–American Express Championship was being played in St. Louis. The tournament was canceled immediately, and I drove home alone from there to Orlando, where I was living. That long drive gave me time to think about doing more in the world, especially for young people.

I spoke to Pop on the way home, and told him I wanted to make a change to the foundation, but needed a couple of weeks to think things through. Pop reminded me that when I was growing up, family, education, and sports were important, but in that order. I knew then that I wanted the Tiger Woods Foundation to focus on education, and not golf.

We changed the foundation's focus from golf alone to something broader, deeper, and more meaningful. We built the flagship Tiger Woods Learning Center in Anaheim, California, near my hometown of Cypress. The area has a high percentage of minority students and a growing population of underserved, low-income students. Pop was in a wheelchair the day I took him on a tour through the Center. I saw tears in his eyes as he watched kids working at various projects.

The Tiger Woods Learning Center—now called the TGR Learning Lab—opened in February 2006, with former President Bill Clinton and California First Lady Maria Shriver in attendance. We now have seven such labs across the United States; the labs focus on the STEM programming—science, technology, engineering, and math—that is so crucial today.

When I think about everything we've accomplished so far, one moment always comes back to me that reassures me we're on the right path. A kid at the learning lab was asked where he'd built a small rocket that he launched on the driving range next door. He said that he built it at the lab. Somebody asked if he knew who Tiger Woods was. The kid said no. That reminds me of what is really important: not my name but what I do to make life better for others, especially kids. It's become that much more evident to me while watching Sam and Charlie grow up. The Tiger Woods Foundation and the TGR Learning Labs are ways for me to give back to a world that has given me so much.

* * *

I've spent some thirty-five years on the course and have worked as hard as I could because I thrived on the battle inside myself and against others. Somebody once said that for a pro golfer, nothing replaces the feeling of coming down the last hole with a chance to win. I agree. That's what I enjoy.

Still, I don't know how much longer I'll play. I do know that I will continue to support TGR Ventures, my umbrella brand, and pursue other opportunities. I think of TGR as chapter two of my career. This doesn't mean I'm retiring, but I am continuing to plan for my life and legacy after I stop playing. I did enjoy my role as a vice captain during the 2016 Ryder Cup, which the United States won under captain Davis Love. This was a natural extension of the advice I've offered to players such as Rory McIlroy and Jason Day, among others. I tell them about my experiences, but I never tell a player what they should do, because every player has a different strategy. Still, if players think my experience might help them, I'm glad to talk to them, just as Marko, Seve, Raymond, Arnold, Jack, and others helped me.

After the Ryder Cup, I spent some time with the guys on the Stanford golf team. We talked about what is required to play professional golf, just as

Arnold had done with me. I spoke about the importance of having a complete, well-rounded game, and understanding your game. You often have to rely on a variety of shots while learning how to play angles, which shots to use, and with what trajectory. I played my best in only about half the tournaments I've won. I had to figure out how to get around the course without continuing to make mistakes as the round progressed. I've been playing pro golf for more than twenty years, and I've learned that it is important to believe in what you are doing. You have no chance of succeeding as a tour player if you don't develop a strong, almost unshakable belief in your approach.

In previous Ryder Cups, I would get my own game ready and get to know the one or two players I would team with. This time, I had a totally different role as vice captain, and I undertook a military approach to my role. Davis was our general, and the five vice captains were lieutenants. I was in charge of the four players in my group: Dustin Johnson, Jordan Spieth, Patrick Reed, and Matt Kuchar. I thought of them as a "fireteam," which in military terms is defined as a small sub-subunit of infantry. They're the guys who go out to the matches to incorporate the tactics we decided to employ. I have been interested in military strategy from the time

Pop told me about his experiences. I read widely on the subject and have participated in some military exercises. It was natural and helpful for me to think in military terms during my role as a vice captain.

I looked after things like parking arrangements, family passes, what clothing to wear each day, how to get from here to there, and so forth. My role included some unpleasantries, such as telling a player he would have to sit out a match. I had to sit Dustin down in the Saturday morning four-somes, for example, and it was a tough conversation to tell the number two player in the world that he wouldn't be playing that match. But that certainly didn't mean he wasn't part of the team. If you're not playing, you get your butt out to the course to support your teammates. He was there Saturday morning at 5:30. As we were together on the first tee to watch every match go out I said, "Dude, this is what it's all about." I was so impressed with him.

I was happy to consult with many of my fellow American players, and I got a big kick in particular from walking with Patrick Reed for nine holes on a cold, windy day during practice. His enthusiasm was infectious. He has an analytical and creative brain when it comes to playing golf, because he is confi-dent hitting both conventional shots and shots that require imagination. It wasn't surprising that Jordan

Spieth gave him the nickname Captain America. Playing every match, he won three and a half out of a possible five points. He lobbied me hard to make sure I told Davis that he wanted to play every one of the five matches, and so I did.

It was fun to be part of a winning U.S. Ryder Cup team, especially because Europe had beaten us six of the previous seven times. I was so into the Ryder Cup that I quickly accepted U.S. captain Steve Stricker's invitation to be a vice captain for the 2017 Presidents Cup. Strick and Davis have been good friends for a long time, and when they asked me to be a vice captain, it was an easy decision for me. I hope to qualify to be part of the Presidents Cup team. But if I don't, I learned at the Ryder Cup that being an assistant captain is a great way to be involved. I represented the U.S. on international teams when I was an amateur, and then in the Ryder Cup and Presidents Cup as a professional. Older, more experienced players helped me whenever I asked for their counsel. Now that I've been around as a professional for more than twenty years, I'm glad to be there to help younger players. I guess this is part of the circle of golf.

I've gone through a lot on and off the course, what with different injuries, changes in the game, and the equipment we use, as well as being married, having kids, and getting publicly divorced. It's definitely been tough at times. Some of the big changes since I won in 1997 are the effects of the twenty-four-hour news cycle and the Internet, which were just starting then. Now everybody has a camera phone, social media, and live streaming. I find myself more guarded, and it's difficult to open up when I'm unsure what will result.

But I have stayed strong throughout, and I am confident in my ability to handle whatever life brings. I turned around the 1997 Masters after my opening nine. Twenty years later, I appreciate even more how much that meant to me. I hope I win another green jacket or two, but even if I don't, I will always remember that walk up to the eighteenth green on Masters Sunday, with Mom and Pop waiting to greet me.

* * *

A final thought: I lived in '97 for that moment when I had to perform. Maybe I don't live as much for that now, but I still crave competing. But I also realize that, physically, I can't necessarily do what I want to do. And I know I'll miss it when I'm done playing tournament golf. Still, I love being on my own on the range and going out in the evening to play a few holes—just me, the golf ball, and the course. *Compete*, though, remains my favorite word, and probably always will.

My parents told me it was okay for me to fail, as long as I gave it everything I had.

I have given it everything I have.

Acknowledgments

Thanks to Mom and Pop for showing me what's important and for standing by me, whatever was going on in my life. My kids, Sam and Charlie, continue to teach me how to be the best dad I can be, and the best person I can be, day in and day out.

The members and staff at Augusta National conduct the most impressive tournament in the world. I appreciate their efforts to make the Masters the best tournament and to improve it year after year. I am grateful for their help with this book.

Then there are the patrons at the Masters. They've supported me from the first time I played the Masters, in 1995, and every time I have played since.

My fellow professionals, especially Mark O'Meara and Notah Begay, have been close friends and have shared their wisdom with me. It's been my good fortune to be able to consult them through the years.

My caddie, Mike "Fluff" Cowan, was an important asset as I played the 1997 Masters. His guidance and ability to say the right thing at the right time were invaluable.

My Foundation and the kids who participate in its programs inspire me. Some of my most memorable moments off the course have occurred when I spent time with them.

I'd like to thank Mark Steinberg, my agent, and my TGR team, which makes me proud every day.

Jerry Chang, Mikey Gout, and Kathy Battaglia made sure we kept things light and easy in the house where we stayed during the 1997 Masters.

Butch Harmon taught me so much. He helped bring out the best in me.

A note of thanks also to Phil Knight, who took a chance on a punk kid as he turned pro.

To Tim Carroll, who gave us his time, expertise, and experience.

Finally, thanks to Lorne Rubenstein for turning my thoughts and stories into this book, and to my editor, Gretchen Young, and her assistant, Katherine Stopa, at Grand Central Publishing. Thanks also to Grand Central's president and publisher, Jamie Raab; associate publisher, Brian McLendon; and director of publicity, Jimmy Franco. I enjoyed working with them all.

About the Authors

TIGER WOODS has had an unprecedented career since becoming a professional golfer in the late summer of 1996. He has won 105 tournaments, 79 of those on the PGA Tour, including the 1997, 2001, 2002, and 2005 Masters Tournaments; the 1999, 2000, 2006, and 2007 PGA Championships; the 2000, 2002, and 2008 U.S. Open Championships; and the 2000, 2005, and 2006 British Open Championships. With his second Masters victory in 2001, Tiger became the first ever to hold all four professional major championships at the same time.

In winning the 2000 British Open at St Andrews, Woods became the youngest to complete the career Grand Slam of professional major championships and only the fifth ever to do so, following Ben Hogan, Gene Sarazen, Gary Player, and Jack Nicklaus. Tiger also was the youngest Masters champion ever, at the age of twenty-one years, three months, and fourteen days, and was the first major championship winner of African or Asian heritage.

He is the career victories leader among active players on the PGA Tour and is the career money list leader. He is second in career PGA Tour victories (seventy-nine) and major championships (fourteen).

LORNE RUBENSTEIN was the golf columnist for the *Globe and Mail*, Canada's national newspaper, from 1980 to 2013. He was the first editor of *ScoreGolf*, Canada's national golf magazine, where he writes a column. Born in Toronto, Rubenstein caddied on the PGA Tour for a few tournaments a year from 1970 to 1982. He has written fourteen books, including *A Season in Dornoch: Golf and Life in the Scottish Highlands*, and *Moe & Me: Encounters with Moe Norman, Golf's Mysterious Genius*.

Rubenstein's work has appeared in magazines around the world, including *Golf Digest*, *Golf World*, *Golf Magazine*, *Golf Monthly*, *Esquire*, and *Links*. The Golf Writers Association of America has presented him with four first-place awards for his work. Rubenstein is a member of the Ontario Golf Hall of Fame and the Canadian Golf Hall of Fame. He and his wife, Nell, live in Toronto and Jupiter, Florida.